BOARDWALK

Boardwalk

A Novel by
JOSEPH KERTES

ECW PRESS

CANADIAN CATALOGUING IN PUBLICATION DATA

Kertes, Joseph, 1951–
Boardwalk

ISBN 1-55022-340-2

I. Title.

PS8571.E766B62 1998   C813'.54   C98-930256-3
PR9199.3.K47B62 1998

An abbreviated version of Chapters 1, 2, and 3 appeared in *Modern Woman* magazine (August 1993).

Cover design and artwork by Gordon Robertson. Imaging by ECW Type & Art, Oakville, Ontario. Printed by AGMV, Cap-Saint-Ignace, Québec.

Distributed in Canada by General Distribution Services, 30 Lesmill Road, Don Mills, Ontario M3B 2T6.

Published by ECW PRESS, 2120 Queen Street East, Suite 200, Toronto, Ontario M4E 1E2. www.ecw.ca/press

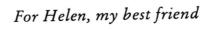

For Helen, my best friend

Chapter One

A few years before I was married, my brother Clyde and I drove to Atlantic City to see what the fuss was all about. Clyde was older and already established. He had a wife and young son and was a senior partner in a brokerage firm. I worked in a camera store and took night courses. The one I was enrolled in at the time was called "Heroes and Anti-Heroes in Modern Culture," and I had along with me one of the texts of the course, Stephen Crane's *The Red Badge of Courage*, in case I got tired of the slot machines.

We were barely out of Toronto when Clyde told me there was a woman down in Atlantic City he thought he'd hook up with since we were going to be down there anyway. And he had that way of talking, too: "Thought I'd give her a shout, see if she's free. . . ." The kind of swaggering talk that's supposed to sound friendly, but always comes out stiff and alien.

"How do you mean, you have a woman? You declared undying love for your wife back in Toronto, not a half-hour ago."

"I just thought I'd give the woman a little dingle — see what was up."

"I can imagine the kind of dingle you're going to give her."

Clyde took his eyes off the road to give me a good long glare through his sunglasses. "So what the hell are you supposed to be," he said, "some kind of Pilgrim?" Now *this* was his natural voice. It had taken only 30 seconds to draw it out of him. I just looked at him and shook my head.

The sun shone brightly as the highway began to curve around Lake Ontario. It was a perfect ASA 100 kind of day, brilliant and cool. Every gust of wind shook up leaves in the fields through which the road wound like a river. Clyde was wearing a pair of those mirrored wrap-around sunglasses the color of gasoline. He probably had a couple of rainbow condoms tucked in his wallet, too — I wouldn't have put it past him. We said nothing for several miles. With the windows shut, Clyde's car was as smooth as air.

"What's the woman's name?" I finally asked.

"I met her in T.O. about a year ago. She was working in a lounge as a singer."

"That's not what I asked you. I said, '*What's her name?*'"

Clyde rubbed his hand over his mouth as he answered, "Ba-law-ny."

I looked over at him. "Did you say Blondie?"

Now he whispered.

"Clyde, what's her damn name?"

"Bunny."

I had to pause for another moment. "That's worse than Blondie." Clyde had a tight grip on the steering wheel. "You're leaving behind your wife and child at home while you visit a woman in Atlantic City named Bunny?"

He nodded. "So what do you want — would it have been better if her name was Antonia?"

"A little."

"Well, it's not, believe me. It's all legs and tits no matter how you slice it."

"So why am I along — can you tell me that?"

"You're here to keep me company. You're here so we can have some fun together."

"You mean if Bunny doesn't come hopping along as expected."

"Yes, that's exactly what I mean."

"And what am I supposed to do if she does — take another room? Wander along the Boardwalk? Visit Park Place?"

"So you know that, eh? You *know* that the squares in Monopoly were named after the places in Atlantic City because the inventor of the game came from there?"

"Clyde, why don't you answer my goddamn questions?"

"You'll go to a movie. You'll take the car and go see Philadelphia. You'll pick willnots out of your ass. What-ever you feel like doing is what you'll do."

"Why don't you drop me off at the next bus station, Clyde? It would be a lot simpler, trust me."

"Eddie, look," and for this Clyde pulled off his sun-glasses, "I'm going to Atlantic City to play blackjack and maybe some craps. Atlantic City is the home of the sweet card. You are going to see the Blackjack Warrior in action. Bunny is just a little sideline — if I see her at all. So relax, why don't you?" He put his glasses back on.

"I'm relaxed," I said, crossing one leg over the other to dramatize the point and folding my hands in my lap.

"Listen," Clyde said, taking off his glasses again, "every-body has a weakness. Some people drink. Some people paint swastikas on the walls of temples. Look at my wife,

Jane. She's an angel, but give her a MasterCard and let her loose in a mall and she turns into a gangster. Have you ever heard of anyone spending eight and ten hours at a stretch shopping?"

"So you're allowed to indulge yourself and she isn't."

"No one's saying that. All I'm saying is that people have their weaknesses, that's all. Don't you have any? Look at you — with your Oh Henry! chocolate bars — that's all you eat all day."

He put his glasses back on and turned to the road again, letting out a breath to settle in for the long drive. I kept looking at him, at his shiny black Elvis hair that swirled around in waves. I closed one eye. If you took an extreme close-up shot of his hair with a zoom, you'd think you were looking at an L.P.

We ran out of things to say after the conversation about Bunny, so I began thinking about my brother. Clyde wasn't a bad guy, really. He was generous to a fault. He was treating me to this trip, and he often bought people embarrassingly expensive gifts they could never repay. Once, for my birthday, he bought me a car — a used one — but a car just the same, and a nice one, an Oldsmobile Calais. When I asked him, please, never to do such a thing again, he agreed and the following day showed up at the camera store with personalized license plates. "You see?" he said.

"Yes, but this is not a gift-giving day."

He shrugged his shoulders. I opened the wrapping. "4 EDIE," the plates read. I avoided looking up for a moment.

"Sorry, my boy," he said. "4 EDDIE was already taken."

"So you got 4 EDIE?"

He nodded.

"I'm surprised you beat out Steve Lawrence for that one, but thanks a lot, really." Clyde didn't laugh but didn't leave either. For the first time in years, I felt like hugging my brother, but that was out of the question. Clyde and I were not physical. The only gesture allowed was a punch on the shoulder, so I pounded him a good one, which Clyde was about to return when a customer walked in. Several minutes went by as we waited for the customer to look around. She asked a lot of questions about lenses but ended up buying only a couple of rolls of film. After she had left, I was expecting Clyde to get his punch in, then leave. But he didn't. All he said was "See ya," and took off.

4 EDIE. Once, when my brother and I were teenagers — well, I was 12, to be exact — Clyde organized a Hallowe'en party to take advantage of our parents' being out of town for the weekend. He bought all kinds of munchies and even baked a cake, for God's sake, using a recipe he'd found in a magazine. The cake was supposed to come out looking like a pumpkin, but it sank somewhat, so it ended up more like an orange tire. Clyde had invited over a dozen people — most of them girls — and he allowed me to ask my friend Leo Bulmer over. I surprised Clyde by putting on a skeleton costume my mother had helped me pick out. Clyde was going to wear a corny Dracula outfit. When I came down the stairs with the costume on, I could hardly get his attention, he was so busy with bowls and with his cake.

"Surprise!" I yelled. Clyde looked at me in his deadpan way. "What do you *think*?" I said.

"You're coming to my party dressed as an X-ray?" he asked.

"It's a skeleton, dick!"

"Oh. OK." He went back to getting things ready.

The party was supposed to start at 7:00, but by 9:30 the only one who had showed up was Leo, dressed as a sailor. "Very scary," Clyde had said when he opened the door for him.

Clyde wouldn't let us touch the snacks or anything else for hours. Leo and I sat around on the couch while Clyde kept sorting through his albums, his Dracula mask flipped up on his head, the evil smile and fangs aimed at the ceiling. Clyde was usually careful with his albums, but this time was different. More than once, he tossed a record half way across the floor when he saw that it was out of place.

I'll never forget that night with Clyde and Leo. I was ambushed by a sorrow so powerful I had to keep going to the can to avoid opening the ducts and embarrassing myself.

In the car, Clyde turned on tapes of Broadway musicals, which was his idea of serious music, and we passed the time, singing along to "I Feel Pretty" or "The Impossible Dream." We stopped for coffee and gas and I took a turn driving while Clyde — still wearing the bubbled, multi-colored sunglasses which made him look like a giant housefly — cranked his seat into a reclining position and began nodding off, just as "The Surrey with the Fringe on Top" was winding down. I gently egged Clyde on: *"I kin see the stars gittin' blurry,"* I murmured,

> *When we ride back home in the surrey,*
> *Ridin' slowly home in the surrey*
> *With the fringe on top.*
> *Feel a sleepy head near my shoulder,*

Noddin', droopin' close to my shoulder
Till it falls, ker-plop. . . .

When Clyde was out, I reached behind me for my jacket and pulled out my tape of *The World's Greatest Arias*. I turned down the volume and searched until I found my favorite song of all, the tenor and baritone duet from Bizet's *The Pearl Fishers*. The singers play two friends, Zurga and Nadir, who meet at the foot of a temple after years apart. They had separated because both were in love with the same woman, Princess Leila. In the aria, they sing her praises to the high heavens but realize she still threatens their friendship. In celestial music, the friends vow never again to let Leila come between them. And oh what a beautiful, musical fuss the two friends make!

I listened to the song a half-dozen times, each time more loudly, before Clyde woke up — just as we were crossing the border at Fort Erie into the United States. Clyde and I both felt an odd kind of stirring every time we crossed the border, though it was true I had already been somewhat stirred up by Bizet. But whether it was by the dawn's early light or the twilight's last gleaming, whenever Clyde and I got to look o'er those ramparts, our hearts fluttered.

All our lives we'd been watching our neighbors to the south from our perch, like voyeurs — watching them play tricks on one another in *I Love Lucy*, watching their big biblical empires collapse in *The Ten Commandments*, watching footage over and over of their leaders getting gunned down, or Addressing the Nation, or debating for all the world to see. We'd read about their Revolution and their Civil War, listened to their Beach Boys surfin' USA and their Bob Dylans blowin' in the wind, and it was *their* songs we sang around our campfires, adding glory and more glory to our hallelujahs.

So it never failed: each time we crossed the border — first with our parents and now on our own — we felt the same flush. Even if we were just kidding around, we still belted out "The Star-Spangled Banner" — we still gazed at the roads and knew they were American. This was America. These were American signs and American buildings and American mounds of dirt at the side and American planks on the houses. These were Al Capone's alleys and Norman Rockwell's fishing holes and Babe Ruth's baseball diamonds and Andy of Mayberry's sheriff's badge pinned to the shirt of the fat guy we just passed, leaning on his cruiser.

When Clyde woke up again, I didn't know how to broach the next subject, so I let a lot of time pass before I said anything. Then out it came in a Southern accent. "Clad, um, ma asked us to stop at Auntie Glad and Sad's house to say heyllo."

"What the hell are you talking about?" Clyde asked.

Gladys and Sadie were our great-aunts — our father's aunts. They were identical twins, alive into their eighties, who now lived together in a townhouse in Rochester, New York, both of them widows of chemical engineers at Kodak. Everyone called them Glad and Sad although neither was particularly gladder or sadder than the other. But Clyde had his own name for them, Hekyl and Jekyl, because every time they called him, or our mother made him call from her place, that's what they did: "*We could be dead, for all you know — we've never even met little Jeffy*

— we understand he looks like your father especially around the eyes, but we wouldn't know — us, you don't ask about — our cataracts, our gallstones — my sciatica," Hekyl would add — "OK, your *sciatica,*" Jekyl would say, *"but what about my bunions?"* she'd add. "OK, *so you have bunions, but what about —"*

"That's why I don't call," Clyde would say. "It's like multiple choice on a medical exam."

"Sorry, dear," Gladys would say.

"How's the accounting business?" Sadie would say.

"I run a brokerage firm."

"Whatever," they'd chant in unison.

Clyde took off his sunglasses, and I could feel him glaring at the side of my face. "I'm not visiting Hekyl and Jekyl."

"Just for a minute. Ma packed preysents fo' theyem."

"Well, Eddie Sue, if you want to visit them on your own time, you can. They don't even have to know we're in the States."

"They know already. They're expecting us."

If Clyde had been driving, he might have slammed on the brakes. He had a brake-slamming look on his face.

He said, "If you want to deliver some gifts, you can. I'll wait in the driveway, and you'll say you're alone, or you'll die."

This was a grand conciliatory gesture on Clyde's part, meant, I was sure, to redress the revelation about Bunny, and I was surprised at how grateful I felt — though why I should have felt that way I have no idea.

Using a map our father had drawn for me, Clyde directed me into Rochester and to within a block of Glad and Sad's house where he asked me to pull over in front of a drug store. "I'll only be a minute," he said and hopped out. I decided to hop along after him. He was — where else? — at the back, studying the selection of condoms and even quizzing the pharmacist, for God's sake, about one pack after another.

I skulked nearby, spinning a rack of novels. I spotted a sexy one, called *Sticky Days in Tahiti,* and brazenly plucked it out. I opened it at random:

> *Fleshy winds blew off the water and tautened Belinda's nipples behind the silver pasties which gleamed like hubcaps in the moonlight.*

I paused for a moment to consider whether or not pasties were like ouchless bandages when you peeled them off but sent the thought on its way in favor of the image of the tautened nipples themselves. A woman and her young son turned down my aisle, and I slammed the book shut. I wanted to replace the book, but they hovered over me for too long. I slipped it under my arm, put on my best Casanova look and swaggered over to the counter where Clyde was paying for his condoms. They were French ticklers with ends on them like a jester's hat. I tossed the book on the counter, then darted out the door, leaving Clyde to pay. I could see the woman and her son lining up behind him. They were studying Clyde's purchases.

By the time Clyde joined me outside, my heart had made a fist and was pounding against my chest. Clyde was kind enough not to say anything to me or even look at me as he unlocked the door and took over the wheel. He studied the piece of paper with the map to our aunts' house drawn on it before pulling out. "Remember," he said again, "you're on your own."

"OK."

"Five minutes," he said.

"OK."

He was holding up five fingers to let me know what *five* meant. I flashed five fingers to prove that I did.

Clyde pulled into Glad and Sad's driveway and switched his seat into a reclining position all in one motion. In another, he flicked open the trunk, so that I could fish out the gifts for our aunts: identical pink velour track suits my mother had picked out for them. I draped them over an arm and held them behind my back. Poor things: into their ninth decade and people were still dressing them alike.

"Any message for Hekyl and Jekyl?" I said through the closed window at Clyde.

He held up the five fingers again.

I rang the doorbell and banged on the door for at least two of those fingers. Finally, Glad answered the door. She was the one with the small brown birthmark on her left temple — but the exact same brass-blonde ringlets of hair as her sister, prepared, no doubt, by the same hairdresser.

She cupped her cheeks in her hands. "Oh, my goodness, look who's here. Sadie," she called out without turning. "Look who's here. Young Clyde has come to visit us at last!"

"It's Eddie," I said.

Sadie came out of the kitchen, wiping her hands with a dishcloth. "Oh, my dear goodness," she said, pressing me to her in a damp embrace. "Did you bring Eddie with you, dear?" She had tears in her eyes.

"Yes, I did."

For identical twins, they weren't too perceptive, notwithstanding their fading eyesight. Maybe it was their unspoken way of paying the world back for mixing them up all these years. Still, this was a stretcher: Clyde had black, greasy hair, after all; mine was red, and I had a freckled face. Here I was, looking out for a single birthmark, and they couldn't spot 700 freckles.

"Come on in, dear, please," Sad said. "We'll get the spare bedroom made up for you. I hope you can stay a few days."

"Only a few minutes, actually."

The two of them had themselves the chuckle of the day. I held out the pink gym suits. "My mother sent these for you," I said.

"Oh, she didn't have to," Glad said.

"Why does she always feel she has to send something?" Sad added, already rummaging at the neck for the label to see if it was the right size.

They steered me toward a chesterfield, draped with a beautiful crocheted cover, hanging down from its shoulders in a V. I peered out the window at Clyde before sitting. There was no sign of him below the dash. I was hoping he'd fallen asleep because he was liable to take off and leave me there.

"So what's going on with you?" asked Glad, sitting beside me and taking my hand in hers. "Is the accounting keeping you busy?"

"*Very*," I said, and I let out a big breath. "How are you two ladies feeling?"

"We're not a hundred percent," Glad said.

"What percent are you?" I asked as Sad took her place on the other side of me and fished out my free hand. On the television set across from us sat a colorized photograph of Captain Mark, Glad's late husband, all set to go to Normandy. A ribbon hung down from a corner of the silver frame. Beside him stood a wedding photo of Sad and Morton, their eyes turned upward somewhere into bright hope. Both women chose not to have children — only their sister, my grandmother, opted for a family — yet these two seemed to love us as if we were their own.

"We've been a little under the weather lately," Glad said. "Some kind of bug that's all over town, coming from the plant, maybe." The "plant" always meant the Kodak plant. Everything came from the plant; it was as if it were God's head office.

"It's made our kidneys ache," Sad said and, on cue, the two let go of my hands and rubbed their lower backs. "In fact," she went on, "we were about to have some NyQuil when you arrived."

"Would you like to have some?" Glad asked. "It's nice and hot and lemony."

"Why not?" I said as I listened to the grandfather clock in the hall, ticking away somberly.

We sat quietly sipping NyQuil for quite some time until the dong of the clock roused me, and I realized that a good half-hour must have passed. "I have to go," I said, bounding to my feet.

I fought my way through a barrage of their objections — *"but you only just got here — when will you come by again? — you hardly ever call — we could be lying here dead for weeks before any of you Marksons would know about it — why don't you bring Jeffy with you?"* But once I was outside on the stoop, the comments petered out with

"Give our love to all, dear — God bless — thanks for dropping in — drive with caution."

When I'd reached the car, Clyde pulled his seat up. Glad and Sad were still waving from the door, so Clyde waved back as we screeched away.

Chapter Two

We drove on and on through the bright, rolling landscape of upper New York State. Most of the time, especially with Clyde driving, I felt I was alone and would like to have read Stephen Crane, or even *Sticky Days in Tahiti*, but I usually get sick to the stomach when I read in a car, so I didn't want to take the risk.

I don't know what I was expecting, but when we pulled into Atlantic City, many hours later, the place looked seedy and dark. Row after row of old gray buildings, many with broken panes of glass, followed streets no wider than alleys. The pavement was crumbling, and even Clyde's car rumbled and juddered as we made our way past small frame houses, their paint peeling and some of the roofs partially collapsed. A few people shuffled along the sidewalks, but for the most part the city looked cold and deserted.

The hotel, on the other hand, was a lavish giant with half the lights of the city blazing from its eaves and windows, and most of the citizens, it seemed, bustling in and out of its polished brass doors. A regal "RI" — which stood for "Resorts International" — was painted in gold letters on the awning. Just inside the door stood a life-sized card-board cutout of Merv Griffin who, I guessed, owned the place or had an awful lot to do with it (because Merv's picture, I later found out, was everywhere). The reception area and lobby were just as grand as the exterior, with signs pointing either to the casino below, the restaurants or to the "Elevators to Rooms."

When we got to our room, Clyde dropping bills left and right to our "assistants" along the way, I realized that the lobby hadn't misled us in the way so many marble and brass hotel lobbies do. The room was as rich as any I'd seen, let alone stayed in. Antique-style cherry-wood chairs and tables were everywhere, chairs and tables to eat at, write at and just plain sit and lean an elbow at. The beds were huge, and brass lamps of every description beamed on with the flick of a single switch. A cherry armoire opened to a television and stereo system with a little card announcing the complimentary in-house movies and music stations we could tune in with our complex remote control. Best of all were the curtains. They were big, thick and green, like theater curtains.

"Do you know what those are?" Clyde said.

"What?"

"They're 'million-dollar curtains' — that's what they're called. Jane and I had some made for our living room — don't you remember? — and that's what they're called: 'million-dollar curtains' because they keep out the sun and cold, and because they cost practically that much."

The bathroom was built to spend a day in. It was marble, floor, wall and ceiling, had a Jacuzzi with four brass taps — *four* for who knows what: hot, cold, champagne and perfume? — and had little packaged dainties everywhere: French-milled soap, scented shampoo, mouthwash, tooth-paste, *hand cream*, for God's sake, chamois cloths to polish your shoes with, disposable napkins and facial tissues. There were enough towels to pat dry an ocean liner, and there was a sun-lamp above in case you didn't want to exercise yourself with a towel. Paper bands hung taut over the glasses and toilet, like the warning tape of a police barrier, and I tore through one after another like the Chief of Homicide.

I left my belongings beside the wardrobe where the porter had placed them, walked by Clyde who stood before the TV flicking stations, and hurled myself backward onto one of the beds. "Hey, take it easy," he said. "Don't turn into a dick up here." I'd forgotten that one of the drawbacks of letting Clyde pay for everything was that it made him the boss. I sat up. Clyde opened a door I hadn't noticed below the entertainment center. The small cabinet was full of snacks and drinks. He pulled out an Almond Joy and tossed it to me. "Here," he said. "They seem to be out of Oh Henrys."

Clyde then threw me the channel changer and set to unpacking his bags and hanging up his clothes. This was one of his most annoying habits. Even when we were kids, Clyde neatly folded and hung everything while I let mountains of clothing grow on every level surface until someone yelled at me. I think people are born either to hang up clothes and tidy up their desks and comb their hair 50 times a day, or they're not. I was content to live out of my bag for the duration of our stay. In fact, the first time my clothes had been folded in a while was for packing in that bag, and I saw no good reason to disturb them.

Just then, as I stared moronically at the channel changer, I remembered how much I loved Puccini. All that Broadway music we heard coming down here must have crowded *La Bohème* to the back of my mind somewhere. I wondered if I could switch on the fancy entertainment center and find some beauty singing like a plump bird. I loved Puccini, the tragedy of it all — the great, dark-curtained swells of music — the million-dollar-curtained swells. I guess I really am a tragic guy at heart. How I missed Puccini sometimes, especially now as I flipped on the TV past the evening news and *Full House* and *The Price is Right*, and reruns of *Roseanne* and *Cheers* and a show featuring a guy building a backyard deck.

I stared at a slide on *The Shopping Network* of a garnet bracelet made to look like real rubies — "so even your jeweler can't tell" — for just $39.95, then switched off the magnificent entertainment center.

When I'd finished my Almond Joy, and Clyde had finished unpacking, freshening himself up and combing his hair, he asked if I wanted to check out the casino. He had on a new shirt and was still patting down his swirls of hair, front and back. "Not really," I said. "Maybe I'll just hang around here."

"Come on. It's right in the building here. I don't mean we're going to gamble. I mean we'll check it out, that's all."

Just before we left, Clyde stepped into the bathroom and pulled a small bottle from his deerskin toiletries bag. It was a bottle labeled "Natural Tears." I asked him what it was for, and he said nothing, which was his way sometimes.

"Do you have some drying of the eyes?"

"Yup."

"And you use something called 'Natural Tears'?"

"Yup. Any objections?"

"No, I was just wondering."

He held his eyelids apart and his head straight up, like someone forcing himself to gaze up at a skyscraper to watch a guy plunge to his death. "And you've solved your tiny mystery now?" he asked, letting the first drop fall into his eye.

"Not entirely," I said. "How could those be *natural* tears? What did they do — hand out pans at a performance of *Madame Butterfly* or something and gather up the tears for their little bottles?"

"You really are an imbecile, do you know that?"

Clyde killed me. Here was a guy who never shed a natural tear in his life, standing here now in Atlantic City, filling his eyes with bottled ones, and he sincerely believed *I* was an imbecile.

He took out another bottle.

"What are those?"

"They're mega doses of Vitamin C — 5,000 milligrams each." He ran a hand through his hair, then unscrewed the bottle and popped back a couple of the chewable gems.

I had a friend back in high school whose name was William Ivory (everyone called him "William" because he hated "Bill"). He was a loner for a long time until he fell in with me and my good friends at the time, Tom Smale and Bruce Bush and a few others. I'm ashamed to say we didn't treat William much better than strangers did. One day when we were drinking in Tom's basement, Tom mixed a whiskey and ginger ale for William. Then he pulled out his dick and topped up the glass with a squirt of piss. I wasn't with Tom and Bruce up in the kitchen when they did this, I'm glad to say, and found out only when William did — after he'd finished the drink and asked for another one. Then Tom and Bruce burst out laughing. That poor sap, William, said the drink wasn't all that bad. When they laughed even harder, William went upstairs to the bathroom to kill himself. Luckily, all he could find in the medicine cabinet was a bottle of Vitamin E pills. He swallowed a good handful before he passed out on the floor. We frantically tried to wake him when we found him an hour later, and when we did, Bruce said to him, "What a way to go — Vitamin E. Look at it this way," he said, putting his arm around William's shoulder. "Tomorrow morning, you'll probably have tremendously nice skin."

"Do you remember William Ivory?" I now asked Clyde as he did his mirror work.

"No."

"Isn't that a lot of Vitamin C?" I said.

"No, I always take them to make me sharp, you know." He winked at me.

"Yeah, but that much? I mean, I'm sure we weren't designed to eat the equivalent of 2,700 oranges a day, so I don't know."

Clyde shot me the imbecile look again. "Come on."

And then came the casino. Nothing on earth could have prepared me for the casino. If only I'd had along a roll of 1000 film, a wide-angle lens and one of those Zeiss tripod jobs, what I could have captured here! "Little ice-cubes of memory," as my boss at the store always tells people.

The room was the size of several football fields, maybe, and had an amber buzz like a hive, but the buzz was dotted by pinging and clanging as if the little flickering starlights in the ceiling were programmed to set off some kind of percussion ensemble. At least a thousand slot machines, which looked from a distance like a crowded orphanage for gas pumps, filled one whole end of the place. As we walked through the orphanage, I saw that all the machines had names: Seven Heaven, Joker Poker, Bar Star, Fireworks Sweet, Gold Rush, Deep Sea Treasure, Hollywood Hills, Double Diamond, Fortune Fortune and the Red, White and Blue. And there was a whole row of slots that took credit cards. I passed a woman whose hair looked as if it were still in curlers who was cranking away at the lever of one these, and a red light kept coming on: "Accepted," it said, "Accepted. Accepted."

A voice over the P.A. said, "*Margaret and Bill Holme, the Number 4 bus to Elizabeth is ready to depart. Margaret and Bill Holme.*"

I followed Clyde past the mini-baccarat to the blackjack tables and watched as a dealer, wearing a white shirt and black bow-tie, spread out a deck of cards before his players, gathered them, shuffled and dealt. He had the white, soft hands of a pianist, but his fingers fluttered more like a magician's. Plastic coins clattered on the table throughout the game as an older man, who looked as if he could have used a shave and some dinner, sat expressionless through win after win. Before I could notice, Clyde had left my side and returned with his own pocketful of chips. I crossed my arms and waited. The dealer shoved the deck through a slot in the tabletop and unwrapped a new deck. The unshaven man stood up, swept his chips into his jacket pocket, looked at me vacantly and left. Clyde took his chair and pulled out some chips. These were no ordinary chips, I must add — no rec-room variety of red, blue, green and yellow — but fancy chips with dashes and doodles and markings of every kind, so that you couldn't run up to your room to the little counterfeiting machine, shoved behind the drinks and Almond Joys, to reproduce them. "Clyde," I whispered. The dealer splayed out the cards.

"Watch the master in action," he whispered back.

I was standing behind the master for over an hour when a scruffy man beside Clyde, who'd obviously had a bad run of cards, turned around to me and said, "What're you standing there for? You're tipping people off about my cards. Don't stand there."

The magic-fingered dealer paused. Clyde turned to the scruffy guy, who'd spilled cigar ash all down the front of his shirt, and said, "You can't tip people off about your goddamn cards. They're all showing."

The guy's eyes narrowed at Clyde. "Well, I don't want the kid standing behind me. I think I have that right. He's bringing me bad luck."

"Maybe," Clyde said, "or maybe you just stink at black-jack."

The man looked at Clyde for a long moment, studied the whites of his eyes, then dropped his head.

"I just don't want the kid behind me," he said, weakly this time, and he looked to the magic dealer for support. The dealer's face showed no feeling one way or the other.

"It's OK, Clyde, really," I said. I'd already moved over to Clyde's other shoulder.

"I want you to stand exactly where you were standing," Clyde said, "and I want to see this gentleman here make something of it. He can call in the goddamn authorities if he wants to."

But the man was already slumped over and mute. He snorkeled his cigar even more wetly, launching another ash down the chute between his arms.

I was a little numb and ready to go back to the room, but I didn't dare to move now. Clyde killed me that way. I remember once, when I was eight or nine, the school bully, a guy named Bruce, and a couple of his pals started shoving me and my friend Sammy around in the school yard over some marbles Sammy and I had won. Bruce had snatched our little felt Crown Royal marble bag by its drawstring and dangled it above our noses. Sammy tried to snatch it back, and that's when the shoving started. I was already lying on my back on the pavement, my heart having turned itself into a motor. There is no other feeling like it in the world: looking up into the spikes of Bruce's eyes, the hatred, the hot moment of power — when, out of the blue, Clyde appeared — I heard the familiar voice before I saw his face. He told Bruce and his pals to find some other children to pick on. Clyde himself was a head shorter than Bruce at the time. Bruce said, "Who's going to make me?"

Clyde snatched the bag of marbles out of Bruce's iron grip, then used it to thwack him across the face. Then Clyde stood glowering up at him, fierce as the jungle, his face two inches from Bruce's, watching the blood begin to boil like oil out of Bruce's nose and jaw. Bruce turned and walked away.

By this time, I was back on my feet, smiling with Sammy, when Clyde, still revved up from his encounter, shoved us both so hard that I lost my balance a second time. "Why don't you two young'uns stay out of trouble?" he said, tossing me the bag of marbles and strolling away.

Clyde could be a real wolf with a wolf's ferocity.

I don't know where Clyde got his daring, but it's a good bet he inherited the quality from our father, Tommy Markson. Our father was a good-hearted guy for the most part. If a moth landed on our wall, he trapped it in a glass and took it outside to set it free. He didn't even swat mosquitoes but shooed them away when they landed on his arm. Any order higher than the insect — dogs, cats, humans, for instance — were another story. I guess they fell into the competitive range for my father and presented a challenge. He wanted to see how fast chipmunks were, so he'd pursue them in the back yard with the lawn mower, giving them a good head start before he aimed the machine at them. He never intended to hurt one, I'm sure, but once, when Clyde and I were raking the lawn, we found bits of paw and ear in among the cuttings. When we told our father, he turned white and denied that he'd had anything to do with the unfortunate creature's death.

He was that way with us, too — not as extreme, of course — but never letting us get a leg up in conversation at the dinner table. If we stated a scientific fact, he'd fill in the other relevant data. If we talked about a year in history that we were studying, he'd dispute the year and run off to check it in a book, right in the middle of dinner. That's just the way he was. And so was Clyde.

I was just about ready to slip away from the Blackjack Warrior when a man appeared out of the blue, grabbed my chin, gently but firmly, and turned my head away from him, then toward him. The man looked exactly like Charles Dickens and dressed that way, too. Just when I thought he'd pull out a knife — it happened so fast — he fished an otoscope out of his vest pocket and shined the light into my ear. "All clear now," he said. "The reddening is gone." Dickens asked me to say, "Aaahh," and was about to look into my throat when two security guards came to my rescue and led the guy away by the elbows.

No one at the blackjack table flinched, not even the dealer who'd no doubt seen it all before.

"That was Dr. Rinjert," he said to no one in particular. "He's lost his mind."

It was almost 1:00 a.m. and time for me to go upstairs. Another hour of watching TV, reading *The Red Badge of Courage*, leafing through *Sticky Days in Tahiti*, and French-milling my face passed before I turned off the stadium lights and fell asleep.

When I woke up, Clyde's bed was still made. I first thought the scruffy guy with the cigar might have summoned a few of his friends to straighten Clyde out but discarded the thought when I remembered all the security people the casino had standing by. I wondered if I'd dreamt the part about Doctor Dickens. Then I remembered Bunny. I went down to breakfast, then down to the casino, where I found Clyde in the same chair, with two other players I'd left there, but a different dealer, exercising his fingers just as magically as the first. The scruffy guy was gone. Clyde was slumped over a little but was still saying, "Hit me," each time his turn came.

"Clyde," I whispered, "I think you should have a little nap and some orange juice or something."

"Yeah, OK," he said, getting to his feet like a robot, sweeping his chips into his two pants pockets and following me out.

And this is how it was to be the whole weekend, with our hours barely overlapping. I left the hotel Saturday and Sunday mornings in search of things to see. I wandered along the Boardwalk, the place that had meant so much class and distinction to me when I was a child. To acquire Boardwalk ahead of Clyde or our friends, to land first on that small royal blue rectangle at the head of the last hallowed square, then to line the rectangle with small, green Cape Cod homes, and finally a chunky red hotel, meant you were on your way to some kind of fortune — even more, the blessing of a long, fulfilling life. And yet here it was: seedy and creaking, the buildings around it peeling like sunburnt skin, small stands selling jewelry and world-famous salt-water taffy, the glum ocean water washing up to it, dark and littered with cups and plastic bags. I checked out a small camera shop, but even here couldn't find anything much better than an instamatic camera — I should have known the second I laid eyes on the Atlantic City T-shirts hanging on racks outside the store.

A few blocks up from the hotel, I strolled along the gray streets, only to find at every corner my heart pounding with hope switching to fear at the strange dark figures who huddled in doorways or sat in alleys. I tried to find a movie theater on Atlantic Avenue, but the only one nearby was showing *Cherry Blossom Gets Plucked*, and I wasn't in the mood for any of that. I walked all the way up to a shady park at the end of Atlantic and sat in the middle of the War Memorial, which looked like a small ancient Greek temple, but when a gust of wind blew through its columns, a dark shape flew up around the back of my head, giving me a heart attack, practically. It turned out to be a man's sports jacket, its sleeves and half of its back burnt out.

I ran most of the way back to our hotel and returned to our room. There was a note on my pillow from Clyde. I recognized the unmistakable scrawl from a mile off. His handwriting was neat and orderly but almost illegible, like an electrocardiogram tape:

Ed,
Come find me in the casino. I need to talk to you about something. Hurry, my foolish little darling.

x x o
The B.J. Warrior

I threw myself back on the bed. I read the card beside the phone: "*All the entertainment in the world brought to you free right in your room.*" I now understood that this feature was aimed at the relatives waiting upstairs, wives mostly, and sometimes children, while the husbands stayed below. I tried to switch on the Radio City Music Hall Rockettes, Live! I wanted them to dance around my bed, but the channel changer was not up to it. It was not until I went downstairs a few minutes later and hauled Clyde away from a roulette wheel that I was able to talk to anyone.

"Listen, pal," he said, placing his hand on my shoulder as we sat at a booth in the hotel coffee shop, "I got a hold of Bunny earlier, and she said she'd probably come by. Why don't you take the car and go into Philadelphia or something?" He was holding up his car keys, attached to his red rabbit's foot key chain. "You really liked that stuff in history classes — remember? — Benjamin Franklin, the Liberty Bell, the whole bit. Here, look." He pulled a wad of money out of his pants pocket and peeled off a $50 bill. "Take this and have a good time."

"I've got money."

"Well, here's some more — take it." He was jamming the bill into my chest. "Buy some Oh Henrys."

"Maybe I should just get another room, or maybe even in a hotel in Philadelphia. It's no big deal."

Clyde hesitated a second, rolling up the bill and scratching the side of his nose with it. "No. Just disappear until midnight — 1:00 a.m., that's all I'm asking."

Chapter Three

As hard as I tried that dark, windy fall evening, the City of Brotherly Love did less for me than I'd expected. Part of the problem was that it took so long for me to get there. I drove past the War Memorial in Atlantic City twice before I realized I had gotten turned around while looking for the Atlantic City Expressway.

When I got to Philadelphia, I stayed downtown until nightfall, waiting for history to come calling like sirens from the city's buildings. Normally, I visualize these things as photographs, but looking back now I can draw very few mental frames around the city sights. What still comes back to me about Philadelphia has little to do with what I saw: they are the images of Rocky, running up the steps of the Museum of Art, or the Philadelphia Flyers, winning the Stanley Cup.

I stepped into an old bookstore and picked up a copy of a book published in 1953, called *Atlantic City or Atlantis? City of Wonder and Merriment*. The old guy at the cash said he'd had that book for quite a while. "No one seems to take much interest in the place any more — Atlantic City, I mean. There isn't much pride of ownership left there, if you know what I'm saying."

"That's too bad," I said.

"We used to holiday there every summer, my folks and I — every single summer without fail. That's where people went. We used to swim and go to beach parties and watch the spectacles. You could barely get a spot on the sand. They had everything there. What Hollywood put into movies, they had in real life."

I ended up in an all-night doughnut shop, drinking coffee and eating cinnamon danishes. I kept fighting off the urge to go back to the book shop to ask the old guy if he'd like to have a coffee and talk some more about boyhood holidays in Atlantic City. He might have thought I was strange, though, so I didn't.

I read some of the book, but stared mostly at the old black and white pictures of the Boardwalk. I got depressed, so I turned to a copy of *The Philadelphia Inquirer* and read it from cover to cover, practically. The only piece I read twice was about a fossil find in Seymour, Texas. There were footprints in the rock of some amphibian they're now calling Seymouria which was crawling around 290 million years ago! How young human beings were by comparison, I thought. Thousands of years, probably — a million or two at most. What little time we'd had to build up a civilization, become neighborly, get angry, then start breaking it all down again. Especially on *this* side of the Atlantic! We were mere pups, scampering away from the hostilities and divisions of the Old World, setting up a free haven, starting war over the issue of slavery, shuttling slaves up to Atlantic City, that jewel by the Atlantic seaboard, then watching them shuffle around in poverty. And what chance do we have to make it through the next 290 million years? How puny were our daily travails by comparison. How trivial whether we get tossed the Queen of Spades or Three of Hearts in this hand. Who cares? Does it matter now that a single Seymouria lounged on a particular rock on the very day his little, green heart gave out?

I found myself wishing I'd remembered to bring along *The Red Badge of Courage* — I was yearning for it, almost — because I'd just about gotten to the point in the little book when Henry Fleming, "the youth," gets what he's been hoping for since the day he left home with his jar of blackberry jam and headed off for battle: a blow to the head.

When I left Philadelphia, I drove along a fairly broad avenue that seemed familiar to me, but the feeling soon passed. Wherever I am out in the world, if there are two ways to turn, I will turn the wrong way. I now recognize this habit as a defect, and yet, each time I'm faced with a navigational decision, I allow myself to believe that maybe, just this once, I'd finally overcome my problem as if it were a rash that had cleared up. I've even checked myself in such situations — told myself that if this is the way you want to turn, then you should go the opposite way — and the opposite way has invariably been the wrong way. I can even be on my way to the camera store, a place I go to every day which is only a few miles from my place, and wind up at the end of some cul-de-sac, waving to friendly people in their front yards, as I take the wide turn and head right back out again.

In search of the route to the Atlantic City Expressway, I headed down what looked like Broad Street, but to this day I would not swear to it, and found myself cruising for about half an hour through what looked like some kind of war zone, with bombed-out buildings and dirty old vacant lots. Finally, I saw a sign for Pennypack Park and got to some dark district of the city where every last window of every building was broken, and the walls were spray-painted with slogans like "Look Taranchoola in the face and Dye!" I decided on the spot that, even if someone were to bring Taranchoola to within three inches of my face, I would strain to gaze at his feet and ankles. I would not want to die or be dyed, whatever the case may be.

I came to a red light at the intersection of two grim streets, rolled up my windows and locked all the doors with one nifty little button on the Allanté's side panel and turned up the heat full blast. A car pulled up slowly behind me before the light changed. I felt my throat tighten for a moment until I realized it was a police car. I pressed the nifty button again, sprang out onto the road, asked the officer where I was, and just as soon as he mentioned Highway 1 and began to explain, asked instead how I could find my way back to Atlantic City.

A second navigational defect I have is that, when someone gives me directions, once the explanation exceeds two steps, my mind goes blank. I'm still nodding, I'm sure, still smiling and watching the person point, but nothing is registering. He might as well have been telling me in Kashubian. I swear, I could have someone in the car with me, bleeding from the jugular vein, and I would find a way to screw up on the directions to the hospital.

The sharp and friendly officer, perhaps sensing sensed this moronic trait, said, "Follow me."

It was 2:30 in the morning when I returned to the hotel. The room had not been disturbed since I'd left it in the afternoon. The card with *"All the entertainment in the world . . ."* still waited on my bed like a little teepee, exactly as I'd left it. I checked the bathroom and saw all the glasses with their police bands still on them since the afternoon housekeeping. I undressed, with the bathroom door closed, washed up, thinking all the while of borrowing a pair of Clyde's silk pajamas, then put on the T-shirt and sweat pants I'd been wearing to bed all along before I left the bathroom cautiously.

I ran to my bed, switched off the lights, lay almost without breathing for several minutes, then turned on the lights again and grabbed my book, which I'd left open on the night table. I read the same paragraph 30 times and, though I'd memorized it by then, still didn't know what it was about:

> *The fight was lost. The dragons were coming with invincible strides. The army, helpless in the matted thickets and blinded by the overhanging night, was going to be swallowed. War, the red animal, war, the blood-swollen god, would have bloated fill.*

Then I heard someone at the door, heard fidgeting with the lock, and all at once in walked Bunny and Clyde. I glanced over at the clock on the night table. It was after 3:00. Bunny saw me first — thank God I wasn't reading *Sticky Days in Tahiti* — and turned back toward Clyde, who was still trying to get his key out of the lock, to allow him to walk in first. It's hard to describe the sensation of the next moment, when my eyes met Clyde's. You would have had to have been Karsh or Annie Leibovitz to capture it — and even then you'd need to be lucky. Clyde said,

"Oh," and acted for a second as if they'd entered the wrong room. Then dread mixed with hopelessness filled his face as it must have filled mine. All was lost. What were we to do now?

"Eddie," Clyde said, "I'd like you to meet Bunny."

I don't know what I was expecting — someone wearing a feather boa, maybe, or a tight, black satin robe that unsnaps at the cleavage and drops to the floor. But Bunny was beautiful, with hair black as Clyde's, which flowed in ringlets to her shoulders, emerald eyes, only a hint of make-up and an attractive, plain, cream-colored dress. She seemed awkward and embarrassed, and our hands trembled as they met. "Excuse me," she said and ran to the bathroom, closing the door behind her.

Clyde rasped in a stage whisper, "What are you doing back so soon, dick?"

"What the hell do you mean? It's almost morning."

Clyde looked over at the clock.

"Did she know I was here with you on this trip?" I whispered.

I noticed for the first time that Clyde was sporting an ascot, for God's sake, and the arm of his sunglasses was hanging outside his jacket pocket. He pushed at the pile of the rug with the toe of one shoe. "No, she didn't know. She doesn't know that much about me, I guess."

Clyde toed the carpet a while longer, then stepped to the bathroom to knock lightly on the door. "Bunny, can we talk for a minute here?"

She let him in, and he closed the door behind them. Except for a bit of whimpering, I couldn't hear a thing. I considered getting back into bed to read my paragraph again but found I couldn't move. I thought of scrambling to get my clothes on and beating it out of there. I even thought of interrupting them in the bathroom to offer to help out in some way. I decided instead to read Crane standing up. I did so for a quarter of an hour when the door opened once again. Clyde emerged alone, ferreted around in one of the dresser drawers, pulled out a pair of silk pajamas and then handed them to Bunny in the bathroom. He stood waiting outside with his back to the door and his arms crossed.

Before long, Bunny came into the room, and Clyde took his turn in the bathroom. She unfolded the blankets of Clyde's bed on the side nearest me and tucked herself into the envelope as close to the edge as she could without falling off. She then said in a tiny voice, "Well, good night."

"Good night," I said. By now, I was in my own bed, pretending to read.

Bunny closed her eyes. Clyde crept out of the bathroom, wearing a pair of black bikini underwear. He dashed across the room and into bed on the opposite side, so that, as the crow flies, I was in fact closer to Bunny than he was. I reread my paragraph a couple of times and then switched off the lights.

I waited for hours in dead, stone silence for someone to snore or roll over or make love or even *yawn*. Meanwhile, I tried anything I could to lull myself to sleep without actually moving, but all that coffee in Philadelphia took its toll. I couldn't very well turn the lights back on, so I considered going to the bathroom to read some more. Then I thought of how sweet Bunny had looked, and I wondered what kind of singing she did and how it came to be she lived in Atlantic City. Was she working at a club here? Maybe she lived in a part of town I hadn't yet seen? Did she ever walk along the Boardwalk between gigs and imagine how lovely all of this must have been back in the twenties when Atlantic City was a glamorous resort town?

These questions came to me by the light of the digital clock beside my head. I remember thinking how precise it was — 5:11 — as the green light washed softly upward into the randomness of the ceiling. It was at that moment, just as I was falling asleep, that I had a terrible vision. It was of Desmond Pencil, a kid I knew back in junior high.

His name really was Desmond Pencil. No one liked him, including me, not just because he insisted we call him Desmond — instead of Des or Desi — but because he had a habit of stopping you wherever you were, in the middle of anything, to tell you about nothing at all — a story about a stupid show he'd seen or about the *laundry*, for heaven's sake, and how bits of Kleenex were always stuck to his clothes because he had a brother with asthma who stuffed Kleenex in every pocket, and Desmond's clothes were always washed with his brother's, naturally, and blah, blah, blah. Whenever kids at school saw Desmond coming, they'd leap into open lockers or skulk behind bushes to avoid running into him and getting the low-down on his crusade against Kleenex bits.

What was unusual about Desmond for *me*, though, was that for some reason, whenever I saw him, something strange and wonderful would happen to me. I know it's hard to believe, and I'm not a superstitious person myself — I once obliterated all the luck I could ever have for seven thousand years by walking back and forth under a ladder all afternoon — but my experiences with Desmond, or *after seeing Desmond*, to be exact, were unusual in the extreme. I once hungered after a girl named Julia Dutton but was too paralyzed by her beauty to ask her out. Then one day when we were visiting a cousin way out in the suburbs, I saw Desmond a few houses away getting into his family's car with his mother. I ran over to ask what he was doing there. He said his orthodontist had his office in that house and was checking out his braces. That night, after I got home, Julia Dutton called me and asked me to the Sadie Hawkins dance.

I thought nothing of the incident until one spring Sunday when my baseball team went by bus to a nearby town for a semi-final game. I shouldn't even have played; I had a history mid-term the next day and hadn't even opened my book. I could answer questions on only one topic, and that was the American Civil War, which I was keen about, but anything else, forget it. I got off the bus in St. Catharines with my teammates, and a few steps away, getting into the Pencils' family car was good old Desmond! Again, I asked him what he was doing there, and he told me that his parents were thinking of investing in some riding stable nearby, and they were there to check it out. Desmond's brother was standing beside him with a bit of Kleenex stuck to the side of his nose. The next day when I showed up for my history class, we were given a choice of only two essay questions — and one was on the Civil War!

Yet another time I ran into Desmond in an unusual place, the Canadian National Exhibition, just as I was about to board one of those whirly rides. While we were on it, something on the ride went terribly wrong, one of the big cables snapped, and my brother and I were the only kids who escaped without injury. There was one girl in particular who was mangled pretty badly. Clyde and I had our picture taken by the papers, standing in front of that wreck of a ride and smiling away for all the world to see.

It was only then that I took real notice of these accidental meetings in odd places with Desmond Pencil, and though I still didn't like him and never wanted to talk to him, I began to hope I'd run into him all the same.

That was what was so disturbing about my night at the Resorts in Atlantic City because, just as I was falling off to sleep, I had a vision of myself working in an office on the 90th floor of a bank tower somewhere. I was talking on the phone to a client, when out of the corner of my eye I caught a glimpse of Desmond Pencil in a three-piece suit, plunging by my window on the way to his death below. In my dream, I hadn't even known Desmond worked in my building. And just to show you what an egomaniac I was in that bank-tower dream, the first thing I found myself wondering — in my office, on the phone — was whether or not it was still good luck to see Desmond in a dream, or did I need an *actual* sighting. The second thing I wondered was whether — even if it had been a *real* sighting — Desmond could bring any kind of good luck when he was plunging by my window to his death. That's the kind of guy I can be — at least in my dreams.

I awoke to the smell of wet hair. Bunny was dressed and sitting at the corner of Clyde's bed, working vigorously with a hairbrush and casting a fine mist in my direction. Her curls of black hair, ringly as fusilli noodles, framed her white face as if Boticelli had groomed her. Clyde was still asleep.

"Hi," I said, hoarsely. "Did you sleep okay?"

"Yeah, fine. How about you?" Bunny was watching me with her head tilted as she continued brushing.

"Like a charm," I said. I clasped my hands behind my head to take a good look at her. She got up to get me some juice from the small fridge and a glass from the bathroom. I watched her pour. "Thank you, that's very kind."

"No problem," she said, placing the glass by my book on the night table. "Are you reading that — *The Red Badge of Courage*, I mean?"

"Yes, it's for a course I'm taking." I remembered tucking *Sticky Days* into the night table drawer under the Gideon Bible. I hoped Bunny hadn't spotted it.

"Are you going to become an English teacher?"

"No, I don't think so."

"Oh," she said.

"I mean, I don't think it's for me. You end up going around saying things like *funnily enough* and trying to find a link between Ophelia and little Miss Muffet — that sort of thing, and I don't think I want to do that."

"Are you taking other courses — different kinds, I mean?"

"No, I'm just doing one at a time. I like mainstream courses, so I stick to those. I steer clear of anything called 'The Horse in Literature' or 'Marxist/Trotskyist Readings of the Marquis de Sade,' but I really like what I've taken so far."

"Is it good?" Bunny went back to brushing. "The book, I mean?"

"Yes, it's great."

"How do you know, though, other than by liking it a lot? I mean, you hear that in school all the time — this is 'great' and Shakespeare's 'great' — but I've always wondered what that means exactly."

"Well, I'm not sure myself, to tell you the truth. I just have a feeling it's great, I guess. I like the life in it. I like Henry Fleming, the character, and I guess I'm taking the course to find out why I like him, which may seem dumb, but I have a feeling that's what all the people in the course do — even the professor. They like one book or another so much they feel they need to make themselves understand it, so they talk back and forth about it. Maybe I'm not making myself very clear."

"Sure, you are." Bunny smiled a pretty smile and said, "That's very nice. Maybe I'll pick up that book at the library and see if I have the same feeling."

I smiled too and said, "It's like loving a song you hear — or sing, I guess, in your case — and then trying to understand why." I watched her as she scooped her brush, a tube of lipstick and a couple of other things into her purse. "Except that music is such a nice way of putting things."

"Like what things?"

"Like, I don't know, like feelings — like love and happiness and grief." She smiled at me again. "Where did you get the name Bunny?" I asked, as she hung her purse on her shoulder.

"It's my singing name," she said. "My manager came up with it. My real name is Penny Lopez — isn't that lovely? Not very suited to show business, really."

Bunny's face unexpectedly took on a look like someone

on the verge of tears, or maybe passion. It's a difficult expression to describe. You'd have trouble catching it even with a camera, but it was an important look in her repertoire, I was sure, a *stricken* look which made her suddenly more beautiful and tragic.

"I'd get a new manager," I said.

She hesitated, then approached me and said, "I'm really glad I met you." She turned to leave but stopped. "Why don't you come by and hear me sing? I'm at the Alhambra Lounge tonight, at the Taj Mahal next door."

"Yes, I've seen the place. Sure, that would be great. I mean, maybe I will."

All of this felt to me like a dream, which blended in with the Desmond Pencil dream, and when I went back to sleep and awoke a couple of hours later, I had to strain to convince myself it hadn't been. In any case, I felt a glow which surprised me a bit, and I tried to picture Bunny or Penny with her brush and purse and that beautiful, stricken look of hers, asking about *The Red Badge of Courage*. Clyde was gone, but I resolved to give it a while before I started looking for him in the casino. I had taken the whole week off work anyway, and my night class wasn't until Thursday.

Chapter Four

I had a breakfast of Belgian waffles, smothered in Vermont maple syrup, with Canadian bacon on the side, and a cup of dark, Kenyan coffee. Feeling insulated and international, I walked over to the Taj Mahal to find out what time Bunny was supposed to sing. On the outside, the place was everything you'd expect the Taj Mahal to look like if you hauled it over to Atlantic City, added a couple of hundred minarets and turrets, then painted each of them a different color of neon. Inside, they'd designed the building like a carpeted airline terminal and added anything in the world you could think of that had anything to do with the east — the Ali Baba Room, cocktail waitresses dressed for the harem, the Marco Polo Dining Lounge and New Delhi Deli, the Sinbad the Sailor Oyster Bar, 1001 Arabian Nights slot machines, the Scheherezade Lingerie Boutique, the Great Wall Gift Shop and the Magic Carpet bank of escalators.

I wondered what would come next? Notre Dame Cathedral, Casino and Nightclub? Carnegie Kick Boxing Hall? Westminster Abbey and Slots with its tomblike machines (so that you could pick your favorite writers or kings and drop the coins right into their mouths)?

The Alhambra Lounge was what felt like a two-mile

jaunt down the carpeted corridors from the main entrance. The sign outside invited us, in big letters, to experience the "Amazing Mike Almond: Magician-Hypnotist Extraordinaire!" There was a photo of Mike, who looked as if he might have run a hunting lodge prior to his magician-hypnotist days, and might have started out by hypnotizing a few hunters. Below his photo was a smaller one in soft focus of the "Angelic Bunny Tremaine," and an even smaller one of another young woman, Pretti Tangerine, whose "piano stylings" we would hear, I guessed, when we weren't being hypnotized. Pretti's eyes were closed in the picture as she leaned back in ecstasy as if pulling on the tips of her keyboard fingers. The show was to get under way at 8:00 p.m.

I felt a pang of guilt when I remembered how much I'd been in Clyde's way the night before, and an even worse one when I realized how much I wanted to see Bunny again. I wasn't even sure Clyde and I were planning to stay on in Atlantic City, but I didn't want to be the first one to propose it.

I left the hotel by the wrong door and walked a couple of blocks before I realized it — though, come to think of it, it seemed strange that the Boardwalk was nowhere to be found. It was there, at the intersection of Virginia and Arctic Avenues, that two cars, one going down Virginia and the other along Arctic, both ran through the intersection, collided with a fearsome crack, backed away from each other and drove off again. Neither driver stopped to inspect the damage, nor slowed across the street, nor even honked or shouted after the fact. None of the other witnesses stood contemplating what had transpired, nor

49

shook a head, nor even glanced in the direction of either of the cars. Only I stood here at the corner of Virginia and Arctic to watch what turned out to be no more than an interruption — accompanied by a sound not unlike that of a cannon being fired — a small rock in the gray flow of life in Atlantic City.

After my walk, I managed to get back to our room for a while to wait for Clyde, but when he didn't show up for a long time, I decided to catch up with him in the casino. I could see him from a distance at the craps table, blowing into his hands and then casting down the dice as if they were magic dust.

"Hey, listen," he said when I caught his attention. (He was always telling me to listen.) "I'm going to give Jane a call later on to tell her I want to spend another couple of days down here — what do you think?"

"Clyde, I saw two cars involved in an accident, and both were hit-and-run drivers — or is it hit-and-run if both take off? — I don't know."

"It doesn't matter. If they didn't care, why should you? So what do you think?"

"I don't know. I didn't get anyone's license plate number."

"Not about that — about *staying*."

"Sure," I said, "Whatever." We had moved over now to another, unoccupied craps table and were leaning on it when I said, "I'm sorry about last night. I know things didn't exactly work out for you the way you'd planned."

Clyde suddenly had this dumb camel look on his face that he sometimes got. "Forget it — who cares? There'll be plenty of other girls like that, don't you worry. I've already got my eye on someone else I've seen here a couple of times."

I shook my head. "I'm not worried," I said, but what a guy my very own brother was turning out to be, spouting gems all the way down here about "hooking up" with Bunny and giving her a "dingle." And now he'd spotted someone else and was ready to move on — just like that. It got me wondering how carefully he'd made the decision to marry Jane, and I was surprised at how angry I felt. Clyde must have sensed it, too. "Do you want to have dinner later on?" he asked. "I hear there's a nice shrimp palace close by down the Boardwalk."

"Everything's a goddamn *palace* around here," I said. "There's the Taj Mahal down the street, there's this place here, now a shrimp palace. What else do they have here — do they have, like, a coin laundry palace and a Nick's Grease Job Palace?" I started to rant. "You know, there are ordinary people wandering around not far from here who are not doing very well even at being ordinary. Have you even been outside yet?"

"Hey, take it easy," Clyde said, pushing me back further from the active craps table. "What's the matter with you, Eddie? Are you turning into some kind of community worker here? What do you want — do you want to go back home? Listen, you still have my keys. Go up to the room, pack and go. You can have the car. I'll fly back."

"I don't want your car," I said.

"Then, what? Do *you* want to fly back?"

"No."

"What, then?"

"I'll stay."

"OK, then. I'll meet you in the room in an hour, and we'll go eat."

Becky's Shrimp and Lobster Palace on Virginia Avenue was decorated with nets on the wall and lobster traps hanging from the ceiling and a big bad painting of Poseidon, which made him look a bit like Elmer Fudd wading into the ocean. Clyde quickly ordered the two-whole-lobster special while I was still studying the menu up and down. But the waiter didn't offer to give me a couple more minutes to decide. He just hovered over me with his pencil and pad. The restaurant wasn't very busy, so I guess he didn't have much else to do. I kept thinking, as I pictured the items on that menu — the prawns, the halibut, the cod — of the Boardwalk and all the things washing up to it. I pictured the local fishermen pulling in their nets and yanking out the halibut from among the beer cans and surgical supplies.

After a good three or four minutes, I finally asked, "Do you have any sardine sandwiches?"

"Yes, sir, I think we do."

From behind my menu, I could feel Clyde leaning forward, snorting almost.

"Do they come with the little backbones?" I asked. "I don't really like those."

"No," Clyde interrupted. "They have a whole group of people in the kitchen whose job it is to pull out the little backbones of sardines."

The waiter was smiling. "All right, then," I said. "I'll have the sardines with the bread on the side. I don't mind doing it myself." The waiter headed for the kitchen. Clyde was breathing heavily.

"What? — Are you telling me you like the backbones?" I said. "They taste like little zippers."

Our orders came out fairly quickly, and there sat Clyde's on a large platter: two red beasts, their antennae and claws poised for action. Clyde donned a bib and brandished a nutcracker as he contemplated his prey. Then he cracked through one of the claws and said, "I'm thinking of changing my name."

"You're what?" I said. "You don't like Markson?"

"Not my last name, dick — my first name. What kind of name is Clyde in this day and age anyway?"

"I guess I know what you mean. After all, you were named after that gangster great uncle of ours."

"He was not a gangster."

"Whatever — the robber baron — whatever."

"He was no robber baron either." Clyde dipped a claw in his garlic butter and sucked out the innards, the juice dribbling down onto his bib. I began operating on the silver bodies of my sardines.

"You think anyone who's successful is a robber baron," he said.

"Did you see the photos of him, with his arms around those strange women who supposedly worked for him? Phew!"

"Oh, forgive me," he said, aiming his nutcracker at me. "I forgot I was with the guy who reads everything from photos. You don't know the first thing about photography, my boy. The best photographers in the world work for *Penthouse* magazine and a bunch of advertising firms. Are they gangsters, too, numbskull?"

"That's the best you can do? Numbskull? Where'd you

get that — from *The Three Stooges?*"

"And the best writers write books like *Sticky Fingers in Tahiti*, believe me. Why? Because they're smart enough to sit on the side of the table where the coins land. They don't waste their time writing books like *The Blue Ribbon of Courage.*"

I rolled my eyes at him. "Have you called home yet?"

"Oh, that's right — change the subject. Whenever you're losing an argument, you always change the subject."

"Who's having an argument?" I said. This was the trouble with discussing anything with Clyde. He talked like a hitter, fouling off balls until he got the pitch he wanted, and then he lunged.

"I don't want to discuss photography with you," I said. "Or literature. You know as much about these things as you do about women."

"Oh, is that so? And what the hell are you? A goddamn virgin, no doubt. Correct me if I'm wrong. The closest you ever got to a woman was last night."

"And how close have you gotten? Tell me something about the women in your life, Clyde. Anything."

We both knew what thin ice we'd suddenly wandered out on and stopped in our tracks. I credited Clyde with good will and sympathy at that moment — both of which I have to say he stored up in ample supply. When it came right down to it, Clyde would always pick me to play on his side no matter how bad I was at something because he couldn't stand to see me sitting on the sidelines sulking. I thought now that he was sparing me an ugly little rehashing of my sparse love life and I was grateful for it. I looked at his face for a glimmer of what I was suspecting, but he had his head down and had returned to stuffing his mouth with lobster.

Maybe, like me, he was thinking of Alice Harron, a pretty girl who'd surprised me when I was 16 by asking me, exactly the way Julia Dutton had, to the Sadie Hawkins dance at our school. Alice's family was strict, so she liked to do things she'd seen in the movies that made the people in those movies feel free and alive. We went down to the railway tracks once and yelled at the passing locomotives the way Liza Minelli did in *Cabaret*. Another time, we ran out into a field after rain, and she made me take off my shirt while she unbuttoned her blouse (facing away from me), and we both plunged face-first into the ooze and ground ourselves into it the way Alan Bates had in *Women in Love*, which I hadn't even seen until after I did all that grinding.

Though Alice was a kind and generous person, she was an incurable flirt. Every opportunity she got, she rubbed herself up against the nearest guy. Once, I introduced her to my friend Leo Bulmer over lunch, and within minutes she was rubbing her thigh against his under the table. Later, when she turned around to get her jacket, she ground her breast deep into his arm. That night, he called me to ask if my girlfriend always shared her breasts and thighs with people, or could he think of himself as someone special. I slammed down the phone on him.

Here I was, courting Alice as properly as I knew how, not reaching for her hand until the second date, hugging her once on the third, kissing her only on the fifth — and all the while she was going around breasting and thighing half the human race.

But that wasn't the worst of it. The worst was the evening she came over to our parents' place for Thanksgiving dinner, and Clyde was there with Jane and their son Jeffy, who was really not much more than a baby then. Clyde joked and guffawed with Alice the whole time before dinner while Jane and I played with Jeffy. Then, to make matters worse, Clyde sat next to Alice at dinner "to make her feel more at home" and there she was, never once relaxing her breasts while Clyde encouraged her to just keep aiming them right at him. It was not until hours later, when I was driving her home, that she let her breasts settle down. I hadn't exchanged two sentences with her all evening, and now she wouldn't even kiss me goodnight when we got to her place. She just hopped up the steps without a look over her shoulder.

Not long after that evening, things between Alice and me began to cool. We still saw each other, though less often, and just as I'd begun to think I wanted to ask out another girl, it was Alice who made the first move. She called to say she wasn't sure about us any more. Apparently, I was killing the gypsy in her. I was hurt more than I thought I'd be. "Do you mean that whole Liza Minelli deal you've been after," I asked, "shouting at the locomotives, and so on?"

"Yes," she'd said. "I don't think we're in love the way I've dreamt about being in love. I — ah —"

She was going to say something important here, and I waited, but it took her a while to get around to it. Just for the record, I wish she'd left it as it was — with the dead gypsy explanation, but she went on to say that she'd looked into her heart "where Jesus was" — that was exactly what she said — and he'd told her that it was time we went our separate ways. It was true I'd realized by then that Alice was not for me. I just wished she hadn't thrown Jesus into the mix with Liza Minelli. But things could never have been too good between us. Besides the thighing and breasting episodes, Alice was altogether too agreeable all the time. She had no other kinds of passion. Sex — or sexual overtures — seemed to be her only hobby. She agreed with everything I said, and you can't go on having one agreement after another with a person. What kind of life would that be?

Clyde was still staring down at his lobster but no longer touching it. "Do you want dessert?" he asked. "They have great desserts here. Come on, live it up. It's on me."

I ordered mile-high chocolate cake, and it sat on my plate like a butte from Montana. I was peering around it at my brother when he said, "I didn't mean what I said about the photography. Pictures are really nice, I think. Really."

"Yeah, sure."

Clyde was smoking a cigar which he did only when he ate in palaces, and he was sending little streamers of smoke upward out of his pursed lips.

"The reason I said those things, though — uh —"

"Why, exactly? Enlighten me," I said.

"Because you're a voyeur. You like to watch because you're afraid to participate in things yourself."

"Don't get philosophical on me, Clyde. Your head is liable to blow up."

"Tell me I'm wrong, then. Tell me what it is you like about it."

"I'm not a photographer, Clyde. I work in a camera store because I haven't decided what I want to do yet. I work in a camera store and show people lenses and tell them the advantages of the 20 to 80 millimeter zoom lens over the stationary 50 millimeter — OK? I like books just as much as pictures — and music, too, and hockey, and mile-high chocolate cake."

"Fine, but you have no explanation for why you like the things you like, whereas I think I do. You don't work in a pet shop, so I don't say that you like animals and should be a zoologist or poodle shampooer or some damn thing. You work in a camera store because you're always gawking at things."

"Fine, Clyde. I work in a camera store because it's something to do. Why are you always on about what it is I'm going to do? Have you ever thought that some people were not designed to *do* anything? I mean, were all of us born to be doctors or lawyers or poodle shampooers? Have you ever thought that maybe we weren't designed to do any of those things? You know, maybe we were designed to hunt some animals and stay fit running away from others and draw on cave walls and sleep under the stars. We were meant to sail the seven seas, maybe, and drown in storms, some of us. No one was designed to sit at a computer terminal in a great, gray, concrete box to trade in oil futures, so some of us may not have found our places yet and maybe never will. I mean, what do we have to *do* all the time when survival is not the issue? Have you thought of that?"

"So that's what it is. You want to be a caveman. We've done nothing right since those old caves when we weren't even walking erect. You know, we may be onto something here about you, Eddie dearest. You live in the past. You cannot accept the present. But anyway, that's not what we were talking about. Once again you've managed to change the subject. I want you to tell me what it is. Tell me why you like pictures and novels."

I took a deep breath, then took a hunk of cake in my mouth. "I just *don't* know — that's the point. I want to think things over before I take the plunge. Look at how antsy you are all the time. I like pictures and books because they help me to take a second look at things. Life goes on, and I'm getting old." I said this through a blob of chocolate.

"You're getting old."

"Yes, I am."

"You are 22 years old — no, excuse me, closer to 23 — you *are* getting on. You idiot." He was waving at the waiter.

"What the hell do you know about it?"

The waiter came over with a white tea towel slung over his arm. "I'll have a Manhattan," Clyde said. "Do you want anything, Ed, now that you're of age?"

The waiter looked over at me. I said, "I don't want anything, thanks, except maybe a cup of coffee."

I went on eating, my mouth gorged with chocolate slabs barely held together by the cake. My dessert was starting to look like The Thing That Wouldn't Go Away. "It makes sense, actually," Clyde continued. "Old people gawk a lot more than they take part in things, I guess." He snickered.

"Look, Clyde, I don't go analyzing you all day, so just shut your greasy face."

"Oh, I bet you don't. Maybe not aloud, but you sit around judging me constantly, admit it. You are a voyeur and you *are* old because you don't know what it is to let yourself go. Do you know what? — You weren't even very good at Monopoly, were you?"

"What the hell are you talking about now?"

"I just remembered — you stunk at Monopoly."

"Stank."

"Yeah, that's right. You'd always just sit there in the game, doing nothing, practically." Clyde tried to blow out a smoke ring, which distorted his face like the bald woman's in Edvard Munch's "The Scream." The smoke ring looked more like a nylon stocking than a ring. "That's right, you were *really* bad at Monopoly. I'd say, 'Do you want to buy this?' and you'd say, 'No,' almost always. 'Do you want to buy the Waterworks?' — 'No.' — 'Do you want to buy Pennsylvania Avenue?' — 'No, thanks.' That's the kind of player you were, and you'd always lose. You'd always try to buy up three little squares so you could put up a house or hotel, but that would be it."

"Well, what's wrong with that?"

"What's wrong with it is that you'd always lose, dick."

"Well, I never wanted to buy up the board — I didn't see the point. I just wanted a place to live."

"But you'd *always lose.*"

"Excuse me," I said, getting to my feet, "I need to wash my face."

"You need a bath with what you've been eating."

In the men's room, I had half a mind to slip out the back way, but I'd left my jacket with the keys to the room in it draped over the back of my chair in the dining room.

When I got back, Clyde was running his finger around the rim of his Manhattan glass. My coffee sat steaming by my cake. "Look," I said, "you're right, OK?"

"What? I'm right?" Clyde said, leaning forward and taking a hearty swig of his drink. "Call in the band — start the parade!"

"Will you just shut up?"

"Fine." He sat back, satisfied, and crossed his arms, the cigar poking upward from his fingers above his other elbow. "Just remember," I said, "that only three per cent of all species are loyal to their mates, and you're not one of those species." Clyde grinned broadly. I sat up stiff in my chair and stared at him for a moment. "I like photographs," I said, trying to be as straight as it was possible to be with Clyde, "because they hold bits of time still; it's like little ice cubes of memory — the memories don't disappear — do you know what I mean?"

"Absolutely."

His eyelids drooped as the camel look came over his face again. "So what do you think?" he asked.

"About *what*?"

"About me changing my name from Clyde?"

"To what? Dork?"

"No. Bob?"

"Bob. You want me to call you Bob from now on?"

"No, but if we meet anyone new down here, just introduce me as Bob — just while we're down here. Can we try it out, see how it feels?"

"Sounds like a lot of fun to me."

"And there's one other thing I've been meaning to tell you."

"What?"

"I'm sick of my life. I've been thinking of going into another business."

"Are you nuts?" I said. "You make hundreds of thousands of dollars doing arithmetic. What business is better than that?"

"Well, I've been thinking of opening a restaurant, actually — back home, I mean. I have a client who has a business printing beautiful menus. He's done the best restaurants in town — you know, Hy's, Barberian's, those places. If you're holding a big, handsome menu, Dougy's probably printed it."

"Dougy."

"Yes, Dougy Ballistrade."

"So because you've got some guy who's going to do *handsome* menus for free, you've decided to leave your ridiculously well-paid job on Bay Street to open a restaurant with nice menus."

"Yes, that's what I've decided."

"Clyde, why can't you stick with anything for more than six months? When you took up ping pong, you needed to be the goddamn Olympic champion, so you asked every Chinese person you ran into if he wanted to play. Then you decided you wanted to become a religious Catholic and went at it with such conviction I thought you were going to try out for the Pope's job — except that we weren't even Catholic to begin with —"

"Do you know what you are?" he said. "You are a simple-minded, idiotic little germ of a human being who can't tell when a woman is spreading her legs for you even after she's dropped her drawers for everyone else." Clyde looked down briefly after launching that salvo. Then he began again, more quietly. "In the first place, I've been in the brokerage business for nearly seven years. In the second place, I'm a wizard when it comes to business — some say a genius — so why don't you just keep your little camera-store-cashier thoughts to yourself, all right?"

Clyde glared at me and I glared back.

"Let me tell you something," he went on, "something I don't want you to forget. I'm telling you this because you're my brother, and I don't want you to stay a boob all your life."

"Please, I'm all ears."

"People are successful," he said, "when they believe in themselves and drive toward a goal. It doesn't matter if they're rotten or saintly. It doesn't matter a damn what their particular aim in life is. If they have confidence, they'll succeed. Why do you have to *judge* people all the time? You'd be surprised how complex people really are."

"You're telling *me* that?"

"I'm telling you that even those people you call gangsters are capable of doing nice things for people. Did you know that? Have you *noticed* anything like that in that tiny little world you live in?"

"Whatever you say, Bob."

Back in the room, I lay on the bed with one leg crossed over the other and watched my foot dangle and wave in the air while Clyde slicked himself up for the evening.

"Does it really matter what the hell you look like at the craps table?" I asked.

"You just never know who you'll meet," Clyde said, winking. He was whistling as he combed his black hair. "What about you? What are you going to do?"

"Oh, I don't know. I thought maybe I'd wander over to the Taj Mahal to catch a show."

"You should," he said. "That's where Bunny's playing. You should try to get in to see her. She's very good." I felt my heart begin to thump.

Clyde was sitting across from me now on his bed. He picked up the phone, took a breath and dialed. "Hi, honey," he said, talking with a bleat in his voice like a sheep. That was it. I decided on the spot I would never in my life call someone I cared for *honey*. "No, I'm just hanging around here with Eddie. . . . No, down in the casino mostly — you know me. The maniac. We thought we'd stay here another day or two if that's OK with you and Jeffy. . . . Oh, you're kidding — there's nothing like your parmigiano — will you promise me you'll freeze my portion right now while it's fresh, so I can nuke it the minute I walk through that door?"

I was sticking my finger down my throat and making gagging noises.

"Hey, listen, why don't you take Jeffy out to the mall and live it up — on me — OK? . . . Yeah, great. I love ya, baby."

As I watched Clyde finish dabbing, brushing and smoothing himself out, I suddenly felt a kind of inertia, felt I did not want to face the ocean air at night. I imagined stupid Jane, accepting Clyde's offer to run up the Master-Card bill. Clyde's hair had begun to acquire a kind of whipped look with all that handling, and I wondered now whether I wanted to be out at all among people with whipped hair.

After Clyde stepped out, I picked up *The Red Badge of Courage* and stared at it. I was startled a minute later by the ringing of the phone. It was Jane.

"Eddie, is everything truly all right down there?" I'd forgotten she used that word — *truly* — all the time.

"Yes, it's fine. Everything's great. Truly."

"May I speak to Clyde for just one more minute?"

"No, I'm sorry, Jane, but you've just missed him. He's gone off to the blackjack war games." I chuckled. "Can I pass on a message to him or get him to call you again?"

"No, he just sounded a little strange, truly. I got a little worried just after he called, and I wanted to ask him just before I went out shopping."

"No, everything's fine."

I heard Jeffy's voice in the background. "Is it OK if Jeffy has a word with you?" Jane asked. "He's pulling on the phone here."

I heard her telling him it was Uncle Eddie. Then I heard him take over the phone, but he didn't say anything. Kids are great. They expect the world just to be there, performing for them, whenever they switch us on.

"Hi, Jeffy," I said.

"Hi, Uncle Eddie. Is it hot where you are?" To Jeffy, traveling meant Florida and Disneyworld.

"No, it's pretty cold. Truly." He was quiet again. I listened to him breathe as he worked on the next statement. "I bet it's colder here," he said. "It's really cold now. I have to wear my winter coat and everything."

"But you like that, don't you? It's fun to have a winter coat on and be imagining the snow that'll fall soon."

"I'll build a snowman, then," he said. "My mom gives me a carrot for his nose, and buttons."

"Great, you see? And I'll come right over and help you the minute that first snow falls."

"I like to build my own, though. I can build the biggest one of anyone I know — Cory, Steve, anyone."

"Well, that's great, Jeffy. So tell me, how was your dinner?" I asked. What a stupid uncle question that was — in the what's-your-favorite-school-subject family of questions — but I was half way in. "What did you have?"

"Veal pajamas."

"Was it good?"

"Yeah. What are you and my daddy doing there?"

"We're playing some cards and some dice."

"Are you winning?"

"A little."

"More than my dad?"

"No, your dad will win more, I'm sure."

"Who're you playing with?"

"Oh, just strangers — perfect strangers who come down here like us."

Jeffy thought this was about the funniest thing he'd ever heard and broke into a wild cackle. When he calmed down, he said, "Can you play dice with me when you come home?"

"Sure. You name the day." I made a mental note to buy Jeffy a game of Snakes and Ladders or Pictograph. I mean, what in hell could you possibly do with a pair of dice if money was not involved — count the dots on them?

I tried to picture Jeffy just then with his father's thick black hair and brown eyes — the same eyes Clyde and I got from our mother (except I got my grandmother's red hair). I wondered which of the two of them, the Blackjack Warrior or the MasterCard Queen — Jeffy would turn out like. I felt sad all of a sudden.

"Uncle Eddie?"

"Yes?"

"Chickens have eyes, you know."

"Chickens?"

"Yes, they have eyes."

"Oh, that's great, Jeffy."

"They don't have eyebrows, though."

"They don't?"

"Nah." I heard him breathe again. "What are eyebrows for?" he asked.

"Eyebrows? They're for looking surprised and angry with. How could you look surprised without eyebrows?"

"Yeah."

"Think of all the extra work your eyes and mouth would have to do without them."

"OK, bye," he said in a wisp of a voice.

"See you in a couple of days, OK, pal? I'll come right in with your dad, and we'll throw around some dice or whatever."

"OK," he said. Then he dropped me to clatter and dangle against the kitchen wall.

I waited a moment until Jane came on again. "Are you still there, Eddie?"

"Yep. That Jeffy's quite the kid, truly." Jane took a breath. It seemed to me there was an awful lot of breathing going on up there in Toronto. "Tell me the truth, Eddie. Has Clyde got someone else down there? — Or maybe you shouldn't. It makes no difference anyway, does it?" She pulled away from the receiver to say, "Jeffy, honey, why don't you go and gather up your money from those little wallets of yours you've got on the dresser. We'll be going out in a minute, honey." Then she breathed back into the

67

phone at me, a big, Toronto, kitchen breath. "He does, though, doesn't he?"

"Not really, Jane. Not that I can tell, really." I couldn't tell Jane about Bunny, not because I felt the urge to protect Clyde, but because I'd come to expect — as Jane herself obviously had, even if she wasn't yet ready to admit it — that even a predictable life was full of unexpected turns, that even Clyde was predictable. He needed a steady diet of adventure of one kind or another. And I for one had trouble accepting the most mundane facts of life. I couldn't look at a Kleenex box without wondering why it didn't dispense the way a toilet roll did.

"I've known your brother ten years now," Jane said. "Do you know that? — *Yes, that wallet, honey, but there's another one right beside it on the dresser.*" I tried to picture Jane just then, calling out to Jeffy, her expression all motherly business, hiding the bitterness that had been there a moment before. She was quite attractive, with dark blonde hair and brown, lively eyes that quickly flashed annoyance. The last time I'd seen her, she'd been wearing a black blouse and skirt ensemble to emphasize her slim figure. But there were always odd little blind spots in her taste because she added to that simple outfit a belt with a huge buckle, so that she looked as if she'd strapped on an airline seatbelt. "And I swear," she went on, breathing again heavily, "I wonder sometimes why he bothers to come home, truly. He's out at all hours playing cards or who the hell knows what else; Jeffy hardly sees him. Once he was away in Nassau on a junket, and it was the third day — the day Clyde was supposed to be back — that Jeffy asked where his father was."

I didn't know what to say. I was all for family unity, but I didn't like to talk people into being unhappy if that's what they were going to be. Still, I wanted to give Jane a telephonely pat on the shoulder, so I said, "Well, you've been together ten years. You must have something going there, Janey."

"Oh, we have something going all right. We have hatred for each other. It's the thing that binds us together, truly, and it's a lot simpler and cleaner than love, that I can tell you." Another woman might have started sobbing at this point, but not Jane. As I say, she was more given to bitterness than sadness and had long ago accepted her lot with Clyde, and knew what that life entailed. Otherwise, she would no doubt have left him.

"Anyway, Eddie," she said. "You're a good guy. Too bad you weren't a little older." I cringed. It was a factor of my age, I'm sure, but my thoughts rushed to the sexual, and I quickly realized that Jane had a face I'd never really cared for, a round, flat pancake of a face. For a moment, I allowed myself to imagine unbuckling her seatbelt and getting down to business, and I felt faint. Even worse, the thought of getting into a bed left warm by my brother pushed me over the edge. All the hotel's Gideon Bibles quivered in their drawers.

I couldn't think of what to say. "Do you know they have million-dollar curtains here in the room, Jane, just like the ones you and Clyde had put up at your place."

"Isn't that something?" she said, and I wondered if I'd steered her away from bitterness now and into sadness. "Well," she said, "take care of yourself at least."

"I will."

Then I thought I heard her throw a kiss into the phone, but it might just as easily have been a bracelet clacking against her seatbelt. I murmured a sad little good-bye into the receiver before I hung up.

Chapter Five

I got over to the Taj Mahal 20 minutes late. There was a doorman I hadn't seen in the afternoon, a very small, older man who seemed kind and pleasant in the way he smiled and greeted me and held open the door and who had little cause to think I was a big time gambler or important in some other way. All I had on were my jeans, a sweatshirt and my reversible windbreaker. I felt like lifting up the small man and swinging him around a bit, but I thought better of it. I was glad to see he was dressed like other door people in what could only be described as a royal blue uniform fit for an admiral, complete with silver buttons and épaulets, instead of some stupid Taj Mahal outfit with a headdress and saber. I wanted to tell the doorman about the double hit-and-run I'd seen earlier but became worried I'd miss out on Bunny's show, so I loped away.

Still, I couldn't help but wonder about him as I headed off to the Alhambra Room. Maybe he was a naturally generous and happy man, or maybe he was just happy to be doing what he was doing. Maybe when he was young, while others wore firemen's caps or tried out their toy stethoscopes on their friends, he was content to linger a long while at doors. Then I started wondering about my job at the camera store and what Clyde had said about it, but I was lucky enough to arrive at the Alhambra just as this train of thought took hold of me, so I sent it on its way.

The room, with its white, plaster Arabic arches, was surprisingly crowded, and there was a guy on stage telling jokes. I took momentary pride in the fact that he had not even rated any billing with his photo on the card out front the way Bunny had, and I was happy to see that I hadn't missed any of her show.

I ordered a rum and Coke and settled in at the only vacant table not far from the front. I scanned the room to see if Clyde was there — I had the strange feeling he had not been getting himself ready to go down to the casino again — but I couldn't spot him anywhere.

The guy on stage looked as if he might have been carted in from the Catskills. He was middle-aged, wore a checkered jacket and periodically pulled at the knot in his tie. I kept expecting him to tell jokes about his wife, but he didn't. It was true this was the tail end of his act and he might have started out with his wife. I warmed to him quickly, especially since the poor guy's photo was not out front and he likely needed the support.

"There's a lot of violence in this country, that's for sure," he said, yanking on the knot in his tie, "but I have a problem with guns. In fact, I'm conflicted on the issue: I believe in gun control, but I also believe in self-defense. So I went to this gun store some time ago and bought myself some bullets but no gun." People laughed a bit here, and I clapped. "Once, when I was down on my luck, I walked into a bank, stepped up to a teller, held up a bullet and said, 'Hand over your money or I'll toss this at you.'" There was a big laugh. "The teller said, 'What do you mean?' I said, 'If you don't give me the money in your till, I'll throw this at you. It can cause a very nasty little bruise.' She said, 'I'm not giving you any money. That's stupid.' 'Would you rather I'd brought a gun?' I asked. 'You respect and reward people more who walk in here with guns and maybe shoot up the place while I have the decency to threaten you only with a bruise?'" Big laughs and applause. "Then once I went hunting with some pals of mine in the woods in upper New York State. We had a bad day, and all we got for our trouble, stomping through the woods all afternoon, was a bunch of burrs on our pants and some black-fly bites. Then, finally, we spotted a deer. 'Don't move,' I said. 'This baby's mine.' The boys held their breaths as I crept up on the innocent creature. Then, when it was in range, I reached into my pocket and hurled a whole box of bullets at it." Thunderous laughter, followed by applause. "I love you — you've been a great audience." He was throwing kisses with one hand and pulling on his tie with the other. I'm sure it wouldn't have hurt his image much if he'd taken off the tie altogether. He might even have gotten his picture up on the card out front.

Next, the host, wearing a sparkling jacket to match the sparkle in his eyes, stepped out and asked that we hear it again for Mr. Benny Littman. We clapped again and someone hooted. "Now, ladies and gentlemen, we have a special treat for you: the lovely voice of Miss Bunny Tremaine, accompanied tonight on the piano by the talented Miss Pretti Tangerine. Let's hear it, folks, for the lovely ladies." We heard it again as Bunny and Pretti walked out on stage and assumed their positions.

I was glad to see Bunny wearing a light blue dress as plain as the one I'd met her in. Pretti, on the other hand, wore a pantsuit the color of gorged pink which she might have selected because she had to hide most of her body behind that big piano. Her hair, too, was a nice shade of auburn when it caught the light, but she had done something to make it stand out from her head, so that she had the look of someone who had been stunned by something. Otherwise, her name suited her if you could get past the pant suit and the hairstyle.

I suspect Bunny's manager had a hand in her program because she sang a medley of almost all the music written in the Western world since the Great War. She flew from one tune to another like a bird, hardly pausing to wrap her sweet alto voice around any particular one. But the Taj Mahal crowd loved every minute. They clapped just as soon as they recognized "The White Cliffs of Dover" or "Tie a Yellow Ribbon 'Round the Old Oak Tree" but had to be quick or they'd miss the next one altogether. They were a sharp bunch, though, and held their own through just about anything she tossed their way.

When Bunny was finished with the medley, which turned out to be the bulk of her program, she settled right down into a stool behind her, closed her green eyes and sang a few Ray Charles songs in their entirety. Pretti rearranged herself, too. I half-expected her to put on a pair of sunglasses for the occasion and get ready to smile a great deal. I was thankful when, instead, she pulled the piano microphone closer to her mouth so she could help out with a refrain now and again.

Bunny began with "Georgia on my Mind," moved on to

"Born to Lose," then "I Can't Stop Loving You." On this last song Pretti helped her out admirably with the refrain, adding a soprano harmony to Bunny's rich, mahogany voice. I felt myself choking up and had to dab the corners of my eyes with the damp napkin my drink was sitting on. I applauded with such enthusiasm the crowd joined me, and soon Bunny was singing a final Ray Charles tune, "That Lucky, Old Sun."

> . . . *Show me that river*
> *And take me across.*
> *Wash all my troubles away.*
> *I know that lucky old sun*
> *He has nothing to do*
> *But roll around heaven all day.*

The lights dimmed, leaving me in a dark rapture. There was a short break to allow the stage hands to set up for the feature attraction, but it took a while after Bunny's act for the conversation in the Alhambra to pick up again.

She and Pretti came into the room through a side door, and I leapt to my feet and waved to attract their attention. A few people clapped again when they recognized them. The two women seemed to be taking a look around before coming over. "You ladies were just outstanding," I said as they joined me at the table. "I think Ray Charles would have been proud to hear you."

"Thank you, Eddie. That's so nice of you to say." Bunny's green eyes were glistening. "Eddie, I'd like you to meet Pretti Tangerine."

I stood up again to shake her hand. "That's a great name. Who came up with that one for you?" I asked.

"My parents," she said.

"Oh," I said, covering my mouth. "Sorry. I just thought it was a made-up name like Sweet Clementine, Cracklin' Rose, Pretti Tangerine, that sort of thing." I smiled broadly, but Pretti rolled her eyes.

"Eddie didn't mean anything by it," Bunny told her. "He's not like that." And when she said it, she touched the tips of my fingers on the table with hers. I felt my face flush.

"I'm sorry, Pretti," I said, but she seemed already to have forgotten. She was busy lighting a cigarette. The flame illuminated her stunned hair, and I could see she was younger than I'd originally thought. I gathered she took quite a bit of trouble to hide that fact, so she could blend into the nightclub atmosphere more successfully.

"So what do you do?" Pretti asked.

"I sell cameras and film."

"Oh?" she said. "Do you take pictures yourself?"

"Sometimes I do. I like to."

She winked at Bunny like an older woman with her friend, having their fun at the expense of the boy.

Bunny said, "He takes English courses as well. He's reading a book called *The Red Badge of Courage*." Then she turned to me. "I haven't had a chance to pick that up yet, but I will." And she touched my fingers again before turning away.

"That's OK. Whenever."

Pretti looked me up and down as though she were trying to place me and said, "I really want to be a dancer, but I can't find work, so I play, but what I really want to do is dance one of these days." As she was talking, she was looking mostly at Bunny. "Have you seen that guy here anywhere?" Pretti asked her.

Bunny turned all the way around in her chair, stopped and looked at me for a moment, then said to Pretti, "No, he doesn't seem to be here yet. Maybe in a while."

The stagehands had set up seats in a semi-circle beneath a banner, done in glittering letters, that read, "MIKE ALMOND: HYPNOTIST-MAGICIAN EXTRAORDINAIRE!"

"Is this guy any good?" I asked.

"Oh, he's amazing!" Pretti said. "You won't believe your eyes. Just watch what he does to people! He's just terri*fin*." She was positively leaping around in her chair, then squirming with pleasure.

"Terrifin?" I said, and Pretti giggled just as the waiter came over with two drinks for Bunny and Pretti and asked if I wanted another. "Sure, but do you serve food as well?"

"Yes, sir, but only finger foods."

I needed something salty to offset the chocolate Titanic which had sunk to the pit of my stomach.

"How about piggies-in-a-blanket? Do you have those? They're little sausage things wrapped in pastry."

"I'll check."

Pretti and Bunny were giggling at me, and I giggled, too. "So this Mike Almond is pretty good?" I asked, directing my question more quietly to Bunny this time.

Bunny looked over at Pretti, then around at some of the tables across the room before saying, "He's good at what he does — very good. He brings things out of people that they have hidden — you know: hidden needs, desires, that sort of thing."

"You're kidding," I said. "But does he do it *for* them?

I mean, does that help them in some way, or is it all for the show here?"

"I don't know," she said. Bunny looked down at the tablecloth and picked something out of it. "It's like your dreams that he works with. Do you know what I mean?" I could not believe how beautiful Bunny was now as she looked up at me — the deep jungle of her eyes in this half-light. I could still hear her singing voice as she spoke. "Do you remember," she went on, "you were saying back in your room how you read certain books and love some people in them, then go to school to try and figure it all out."

"Yes."

"Well, this is a little like that. Mike — Mike Almond, I mean — goes straight there — to that dream part, that part you can't explain, and opens it up for you."

"On stage."

"Yes, on *stage*," she said irritably and turned away from me.

The glittering host was now at the microphone again. He made his voice somber and deep: "Ladies and gentlemen, you are about to witness one of the great acts of our time, the great Mike Almond, hypnotist-magician *extraordinaire!*" There was sporadic clapping around the room. "You'll need to do better than that, ladies and gentlemen. The great Almond needs encouragement. Let's all put our hands together and call out to him! Mike, Mike, Mike, Mike. . . ."

People hesitated, but then smiled at their companions as the call for Mike picked up steam. "Mike, Mike, Mike, MIKE, MIKE! MIKE! MIKE! . . . ." It was not until most of the room had joined in that, suddenly, a surprisingly small figure from out of the darkness somewhere leapt into the spotlight. He was dressed all in black, except for the white letters on his tee-shirt, done in an arc like his sign and proclaiming, "The Great Almond!" He was a short but muscular man with longish brown hair that shone in the stage light. I remembered his hunting lodge pose in the photo out front. He raised his strong, veiny arms as the chant, led by the phantom announcer, drubbed on. "MIKE! MIKE! MIKE! MIKE!"

Then Mike stretched out his arms, like a religious figure. "Thank you," he said into the microphone, emphasizing the depth of his own voice.

A net of silence fell over the big room.

"Thank you," he said again. "It's great to be here in Atlantic City. I love to work these great establishments like the Taj Mahal." Mike Almond raised his arms again, then dropped them, clasping his hands in front of him. "Now, gentle folk of Atlantic City," he went on, his voice deep and mellow in the microphone, like an FM announcer's, "I'm going to call upon some of you to volunteer up here on this platform, but before I do, I want to remind you all that hypnosis is not harmful in the hands of a *trained* hypnotist, so I don't want you to try it on your pals and relatives — well, not your pals anyway." Laughter. "I want to say just one more thing before we begin on this fine fall evening." He raised a cautionary finger. "You cannot hypnotize a person to do what he or she does not want to do — like commit murder — unless, of course, we get a murderer up here." A great burst of laughter. "And a person will not be hurt by this experience. Some of you out there *cannot* be hypnotized, so I ask you all, please, to bear with me. Not all of you will be eligible."

The waiter brought in my piggies-in-a-blanket. I felt a burst of gratitude for his trouble and jumped to my feet to hand him a few dollars.

"What's going to happen now?" I asked, back in my seat.

"Just wait," Bunny said. "He's going to pick the people he thinks will be easiest to hypnotize. He really is amazing. Just watch."

Pretti squealed into a giggle before taking a swig of her drink.

"Does he ever do magic?"

"Not lately, I don't think. This show of his has been a hit, so I think he'll stick with it for a while."

The club had grown quite noisy. Scraps of nervous laughter arose all around the room as people conferred with their neighbors. Within a few minutes there were a couple of dozen volunteers standing before Almond at the foot of the platform, giggling with one another, looking nervously back at their tables in the darkness.

One table in particular, a few down from us, held what looked like a group of Scottish highlanders — lads and lasses both — in town for their own show, probably. They were got up in full regalia: kilts on the men, bagpipes at their sides on the floor. They were all chanting, "MacTeague, MacTeague, MacTeague," at one of their compatriots standing up there with Almond.

Within minutes, Mike Almond had cut his list of people to eight, and they joined him on stage. He had his back to us and was speaking quietly to the group, a small spotlight over his shoulder bringing each of the faces into focus, then out of it as he wagged his upper body, using his shoulder as a black screen. Very quickly, half the volunteers were rejected, one after another, until only four remained.

Pulling the microphone from its stand, Almond said, "Ladies and gentlemen, I think we're all set now." He turned toward his small, select group. "Would the four of you stand up, please?" Almond dropped the microphone to his side and said something to each of them, using his shoulder again to block and unblock the light reaching their faces. He had to stand on tiptoe for MacTeague.

Then he raised the microphone again. "I want you all, now, to straighten out your arms and press your hands together with whatever force you can muster." He demonstrated, clapping a boom into the microphone. His arms shone in the light. "Press, press, press," he said. "And now —" he raised his arm in the air like a conductor — "you cannot separate those arms again. Try, try!" The arms were stuck together. "Separate them, separate them!"

Howls of laughter blew over the audience. Pretti hooted and clapped. Almond spoke again, without benefit of the microphone, to his four volunteers. Their eyes rolled back and the lids closed, as he turned once again toward us. The FM voice said, "I think we're all set now. Lisa," he continued without looking back at her, "come over here, darling." Lisa's eyes flickered open as she joined Almond at the microphone. She was a scruffy, small girl, who wore her wavy brown hair tied in a ponytail, and had long and squiggly earrings. She was being cheered on by a whole table of scruffy girls not far away from us. I took a small, flaky bite out of one of my piggies and felt a stitch at my side.

"What is your name, darling?"

Lisa held her hands clasped in front. "Lisa — Lisa Vaughan."

"Well, Lisa Lisa Vaughan" — laughter — "are you rich in your dreams?"

"Um, I'm not sure what you mean." Lisa swayed slightly, back and forth. She had a glazed look in her eyes.

"We'll see," he said. "Lisa, what are the magic words I taught you a few minutes ago?"

"Key in."

"Yes. When I say those words to you, you *won't* remember your name. You got that?"

"Yes."

"OK, let's try."

"OK." Her voice was small and metallic in the microphone.

"Key in. Lisa, what's your name?"

"Pardon?"

"Lisa, I want to know your name."

"*My* name?"

"That's right, Lisa."

"Um."

Delight rumbled over the big room. "Now, Lisa, do you remember how I bring you out of this?"

"You snap your fingers."

Almond snapped. "What is your name?"

"Lisa Vaughan."

"Pardon?" Almond smiled at the crowd as his black eyes surveyed the room.

"What was your question?" she asked.

"My *question?*"

"Didn't you ask me a question? I thought —"

"I asked you your name."

"Oh — it's Lisa Vaughan."

"Thank you, Lisa." Almond raised his arm to the warm applause, and Lisa smiled, hooding her eyes from the light and waving at what sounded like a whole bus tour of friends. "Now, Lisa, do you still remember the magic words?"

"Key in."

"That's right. But this time I'm not going to snap my fingers to bring you around. This time, I'm going to say 'key *out*' to wake you up. You got that?"

"Yes, key out." Lisa giggled.

"When I say the magic words now, Lisa, you're going to become very rich. Key in. Lisa, what is that piece of paper you're gripping there in your hand? Is that a lottery ticket?"

She gazed down at her empty hand. "Yes, it's a ticket."

I looked over at Bunny and groaned, "Oh, no," and felt the stitch at my side spread across my abdomen. But Bunny was too captivated by the show to notice me.

Almond said, "Lisa, honey, turn on your TV there." Lisa held back her bangs as she leaned forward to switch on the phantom TV. "Lisa, the largest jackpot in the history of the world is about to be given away: you ready? — one *hundred* and twenty-five *million* dollars. You are watching the lottery results on that TV and holding your ticket. Your hands are sweaty." Almond took one of Lisa's hands, then nodded and smiled at the audience, which roared its approval. "Your ticket, Lisa, my love, says, '1, 7, 17, 27, 37 and 47,' the same weird numbers you pick each week." Lisa laughed and nodded and the crowd laughed, too.

"You ready?" She was still nodding and now biting her lower lip. "The announcer," Almond droned into the mike, "is pulling the first feathery ball out of that windy cage, Lisa. It's a 47." Lisa stared into the darkness at the vast television that was the audience. "The next number's a 17!"

"Free ticket!" Lisa yelped as the crowd roared.

"Now a 7, now a 37 . . . and now . . . a 1."

"Oh, my God." Lisa pulled on her bangs with one hand and held her ticket to her heart with the other. Her swinging earrings picked up the glint of the lights.

" 'Dang these squirrely little balls,' the announcer says. 'We need one more to drop.' Lisa, that last ball has just dropped, and even before the announcer has had a chance to call it out, your eyes light on it. It's a 27."

Lisa's eyes filled with tears. Her friends applauded. She gripped the ticket to her face and poured kisses on the hands that held it, then dropped to her knees, got hold of one of Almond's hands, smothered it with kisses and let out a wail from a place so deep in her small frame it seemed to come from another part of the hotel. The wail doused the laughter in the large room, and a chilling silence fell. Lisa dropped backward with a thud, her chest convulsing, and raised her legs in the air the way a dog does. I could feel my eyes brimming with tears and ran my shirt sleeve over them before anyone noticed.

Mike Almond said, "Key *out.*"

Lisa rolled onto her side to face the audience, a couple of the clips in her hair having fallen out, the ponytail off-center. Her grip loosened. Even in the distance I could see blood in one of her palms. Then Lisa saw her friends. She looked as if a thousand people had come to wake her up in the morning. The silence held. Lisa scampered on all fours to her seat and pulled herself up, her stunned face buried in her hands. It was then she saw the blood and cried out.

"Can I get a little hand up here?" Almond said. He escorted Lisa to the edge of the platform where a couple of her friends met her, offered her a napkin and led her back to her seat in the darkness.

I leaned forward toward Bunny and said, "Would you like to go somewhere else? I'd be glad to buy you a drink — both of you. What do you think?"

"No, why don't we stay, Eddie? Lisa will be all right, you'll see." She patted my hand. "It was a dream to Lisa, that's all. Mike does this all the time to people."

Pretti laughed and Bunny joined in. Frost ran over my spine, and I shuddered. But Bunny kept her eyes on me as I crossed my arms, and she smiled.

"Now, who do we have next?" Almond asked, waving his hand behind him at the other three on stage. The hoots and whistles over my shoulder from the Scottish table were worthy of the highlands where they'd emboldened their hooters. MacTeague smoothed out his kilt and stood erect.

"And you are Robert?" Almond asked, holding the microphone up to the highlander's mouth.

"Yes, Robert MacTeague."

"Very nice."

"Thank you, yes."

"You're quite a brawny guy there, Robert." Hoots and laughter.

"Thank you, yes. I try to keep in shape. I work out in a wee gym buck home."

Robert was shifting his weight now from foot to foot, then shading his eyes to locate his friends. "Is it true what they say," Almond droned, "that you folks wear nothing under these things?" He gave Robert's kilt a tug.

"It as," Robert said. "It as a tradition in Scote-lund."

"We'll soon see." Shouts and whistles. "What are the sweet words for us this evening, Robert?"

"They're *key an*," Robert said, craning his neck to speak deep into the microphone.

"Yes, key in, Robert." The highlander stood expressionless. "Robert, you are the United Kingdom's best hope to medal in gymnastics at the next Summer Games. Your *very* best routine," Almond said as he shifted the microphone stand to the side, "is the floor exercise — you got that?"

"Aye," Robert said, clapping his hands together.

"You are now back at your wee gym, getting ready for those Games. Get ready, Robert, get *ready*. You have only six weeks left before you head off to the Olympics!"

Robert marched to one end of the platform, stood tall, then flew across the stage in a cartwheel — not a bad one at that. At the opposite end of the stage, huffing and earnest, he raised himself into a handstand, and his kilt fell down over his chest and face. His genitals dangled upside-down and quivered like fruit in a wind as Robert manfully held his balance for a good, long minute, the crowd guffawing, the highlander table screeching and whistling like tea kettles.

"*Very* nice," Almond said as he tapped Robert on the ankle. "Take five now and sit here beside our next participant."

Robert crumpled up into his kilt and scampered, amid shrieking applause, to a chair at the back.

Prancing like a diva, Almond then escorted into the light a stocky, middle-aged man whose sports jacket was too tight on him. The remaining specimen, behind them, was slumped in her chair, and she seemed to be asleep.

"And you are — ?"

"Stanley Mills."

"Stanley," Almond said, laying a hand on the man's shoulder, "If you had your druthers, what would you be? In other words, what would you be if you could be anything in the world or *anybody*, past or present?"

Stanley grunted into the microphone, then said, "I'd like to be an artist. I wish I could have been Picasso. His work, called 'Guernica,' is so magnificent that it —"

"*Fine*, Stanley," Almond said, pulling away the microphone. "We don't need an art history lesson here." Laughter. I looked all around me. Stanley didn't seem to have a table rooting for him. "You want to be an artist? So you shall be. What words are critical for us here today?"

"Key in."

"That's exactly right. When I say those words, you shall be the world's greatest artist. Key in now, Stanley." Almond moved Stanley to the front of the platform, then withdrew, leaving him to stand alone in the spotlight. "Stanley, you are *now* the world's greatest artist. You *are* Picasso, Stanley, my man. What you have before you is a giant canvas. Buyers in New York, London and Paris await your every brush stroke — every stroke worth a thousand dollars." Stanley was already mixing colors on his invisible pallet, squeezing out a bit more from a tube of paint.

"Paint, Stanley! Paint!" Almond shouted, and Stanley wielded his magic brush and stroked broadly across the canvas. Then a powerful circle. He stepped back, put a hand on his chin. His face was pinched in concentration. The crowd roared. He placed a hand on his hip while with the other he dabbed in some detail.

Almond stepped up into the bright light. "While Stanley is finishing his masterpiece for us, let's call upon — was it Catherine?" Catherine stood up on her own. "Oh-oh," Almond said, "Let's move Stanley off to the side here out of the way."

He led Stanley off into the shadows. Catherine was shaking her head and saying something that no one but Almond could hear. He hid the microphone behind his back. It wasn't until Catherine scooted to the edge of the platform and down the stairs that Almond spoke into the mike. "Oh, we have an unwilling lady. We must have awakened her at the wrong time. Let's have a hand for Catherine anyway." People applauded as Catherine joined what looked like her parents and maybe a sister or friend. She stood again to wave. "So all we have working away here is Pablo." Stanley angrily splashed paint on the air.

Robert MacTeague stepped into the light, snorted like a bull, and once again stood on his hands. During his rest, Robert had acquired a stout erection — one he could be quite proud of — which he now aimed at the audience like a weapon. The crowd slid into hysteria. Almond folded Robert up and whispered into his ear so that the man resettled, zombie-like, into his seat.

"Can I please have one more volunteer?" This time people were not as forthcoming as before. "*Anyone?*" Almond said.

Bunny looked over at Pretti, and the two women giggled. Bunny took a big gulp of her drink and got to her feet. I pulled on her arm. "You can't. You, of all people. You were in the show. You just can't."

"Please, Eddie, it's for *fun*," she said, trying to free her arm. I tightened my grip. "Do you think I shouldn't?" She was crouching now, half-ready to sit back down.

Pretti giggled again. "Ah, go for it," she said. "You're not jumping out of a plane. Go for it." Pretti looked at me coldly and snapped, "Why don't you just leave her the hell alone!" I was taken aback.

"Will you come with me?" Bunny asked her.

"No, I went last night. It was great. I danced like a swan."

"I'll go with you," I said.

"You will?" I nodded and she took my hand. And then I hesitated as I quickly imagined myself up there like a robot. "Are you afraid?" Bunny said as her grip loosened around my hand. "Are you afraid of your dreams?"

"No, but I do my best dreaming in a bed, really. You must admit, this is a little revolting." Bunny just smiled at me.

I don't know for sure what took possession of me, but I decided that, if Bunny was going up there to make a fool of herself, I could be a fool too. So I stood up firmly and followed. Maybe Almond had an idiotic routine for couples he could draw out of us.

When it became apparent to the crowd that it was Bunny who was volunteering to become the next guinea pig, people gave her a bigger ovation than they had for her singing.

"Well, who do we have here?" Almond said. We were at the foot of the stage. "It is the lovely Bunny Tremaine. What a sport you are, sweetheart."

89

"And I'm Eddie Markson," I said, looking up at the muscular little hunting lodge operator.

With a look of glee, Bunny lolloped up the stairs at the side of the small stage. Almond meanwhile leapt down and stared for a good long moment into my eyes. "You cannot be hypnotized," he said.

"Sure, I can. Why not?"

"Because some people can't surrender themselves up to it, that's all. I can tell, believe me." He turned and with a little springing motion vaulted up onto the platform.

Bunny looked down at me and mouthed the words, "It's OK."

"Well, how do you know *she* can?" I yelled up at Almond, but he pretended not to hear. I felt ridiculous as I checked behind me at what the crowd thought of all this. I hated being the center of attention, so I skulked back in the direction of my seat. For a second, I had trouble finding it because Pretti was no longer at our table.

The room was now calling out and clapping in rhythm for "Bunny! *Bunny! Bunny!*"

Almond raised his arm to settle the crowd, replaced the microphone on its stand, and using his shoulder again to direct the light, laid his hands on Bunny's cheeks and looked into her eyes in the way an ophthalmologist would. He spoke to her for a few moments, then took her to a vacant chair a couple over from Robert and knelt before her. The lids of her eyes closed like drapery.

Almond stepped up to the mike once again. "I believe we have a new and lovely dreamer." He fetched Bunny and helped her to the front. Then came the voice from FM: "You, of course, remember the magic words, Ms. Tremaine."

"Yes," she said, looking down and brushing an invisible speck from her blue dress.

Bunny looked striking in the bright spotlight. I realized suddenly that my knees were trembling. Almond had his arm around her waist. Stanley, behind them, had pulled over a chair and now stood on it, painting the top of his canvas.

"Key in," the voice breathed, not a half-inch from the microphone. Bunny's face was solemn. "How lucky we are to have saved the best to last," Almond droned, and the crowd answered with hoots and more clapping.

"Bunny," Almond said, "you are back in high school, a shy girl but — though you would never admit such a thing to yourself — the prettiest in the building. For the very first time in your life, my dear, you have fallen deeply and hopelessly in love with a boy, whose name is Frank. He is tall, handsome and popular — so popular that you are sure he's never noticed the pretty face and sparkling eyes behind the plain-Jane look you have worn all your life. You have noticed him, and whenever you can, you have watched him from a distance. You are mad to embrace him."

Bunny looked down and studied her feet as if being asked a difficult question by a quiz-show host. As she gazed up, she began slowly and deliberately to raise her arms and cross them, so that each of her hands finally settled on the opposite shoulder. I felt my heart flutter. Almond, meanwhile, spotted a table not far from me which had a large fruit and cheese platter on it and called for a piece of fruit. A smiling young man walked to the edge of the platform and handed Almond a rosy apple. Almond returned to Bunny's side.

"The morning you have your first encounter with young Frank you are getting ready for school, standing in the shower thinking about him this morning the way you did when you fell asleep. The warm water flows down your shoulders and over your breasts —"

Bunny ran her hands down from her shoulders to her hips and then upward across her chest. I could see the nubs of her nipples sprouting through her blue dress and felt ready to lunge up at her, to tear her away from this hunting-lodge goon. She lifted her hands heavenward to the shower's spout. "Your hands trail down over the ribs that constrain your breathing, but you must move on now. You get out because it's running late, pat yourself dry and put on a light flower-print dress and no bra." Bunny went through the motions by raising her arms in the air, the straps of her dress slipping down until they hooked onto her shoulders.

A spring formed in my knees. I was sick to my stomach. I wanted to bolt to the stage, but I was paralyzed. My eyes were drawn to the luster of Bunny's form in the spotlight, and I remained pinned to my chair. Bunny had the glow of a star — even more radiant now than when she sang "Georgia on my Mind" — and I found myself attracted and repelled in equal measure.

"Bunny," Almond said, "you are now at school, and you are mad to embrace Frank." He handed her the apple, and she brushed her cheek against it. "You are mad just to talk to him, to watch the shape of his words on his lips." Bunny began now to drag her fleshy lower lip along the surface of the apple.

"You want to pull a loose thread from the cuff of his

92

jacket and brush the palm of his warm, dry hand as you do so." Bunny pulled on the woody stem of the apple. The audience was stone silent.

"You are now at your locker at one end of the long hall, and he is at the other, chatting to two other girls in cheerleader's outfits. He glances up and notices you. Your heart races, you gulp air. He has taken a step toward you, and you toward him. Now he is walking quickly. His shadow is upon you. His face, as you look up, blocks out the light above his head. 'Hi,' he says."

Bunny said, "Hi," and some people laughed, but Almond snapped an imperious hand in the air, restoring calm. Stanley Picasso was now sitting in his chair, contemplating his opus.

"'I love you, Bunny.' These are the very first words he addresses to you. Imagine. 'I love you.' You can feel your warm skin beneath the thin cloth of your dress. 'I want to kiss you.'"

"What, here in the hall?" Bunny said to her apple. She was swaying a little.

"'Kiss me,' he says, as he circles you, sleek as a panther, his breath upon you. He stops, his face an inch from yours." Bunny licked the apple before biting into it gently, holding the morsel in her mouth, not chewing. "Oh, Bunny," Almond said, his voice breathy and faint. She was swaying helplessly now, teetering toward the edge of the platform. Almond took her arm to prevent her from falling off. The crowd remained silent. Some people, I could see, were swaying with Bunny, as if to a fragrant melody. Without benefit of the mike, people could hear Bunny moan as her body waved before them. The ceiling had opened to starry heaven. Bunny's moan became a hum, sweet and sad. She had that look about her again, the one I'd seen the morning before in our hotel room, the stricken look of someone caring for a sick child, maybe, but heated up to a passion.

I felt myself becoming light-headed as I got caught up in the drowsy swing of the room. I thought this was the story that people in the Alhambra would tell long after their visit to Atlantic City. They would talk about the night they watched a pretty woman sway in her dreams while the whole world watched.

Mike Almond let Bunny carry on for several quiet minutes. She sat down in the spotlight, still swaying and humming, still embracing her apple. Almond walked over to poor Stanley and snapped his fingers in his ear. Then he whispered in Robert's ear. The two were given a small cheer as they came to, and Stanley waved out at the audience. Then he noticed Bunny and sat back down in his chair behind her to watch quietly. Robert rejoined his highlanders, studying their meek, giggly faces, before he too turned to watch Bunny.

I now got to my feet and walked boldly toward the stage, where I stood, arms crossed, waiting for Almond to snap Bunny out of her reverie, but he released her instead, raising a finger to his lips, helping her to her feet and handing her over to the glittering host who suddenly appeared from the side somewhere and guided Bunny off the stage.

I edged back to my seat. Pretti was gone. It was as if a spell had been cast over the Alhambra. There was no applause in the room and no conversation. We all waited for something to happen.

Finally, the host returned and held his arm up in the air: "Mike Almond, ladies and gentlemen." And then the room exploded in its appreciation. The small, muscular man dressed in black gave a deep and athletic bow, ran off stage, leaving Stanley still sitting awkwardly in his chair. In a few seconds, he sprinted back out to release him, got a big laugh, waved again and jogged off stage for good.

I sat for a long time, finished my drink, which had become watery with the melted ice, settled up with the waiter, then lingered a while longer, hoping Bunny would appear from backstage. When she didn't, I panicked.

Chapter Six

I hunted so long for Bunny up and down the corridors backstage that I began to believe that her disappearance was the magic part of Almond's act. I finally came upon a row of rooms with stars on the doors. I knocked on the first, and when no one answered, entered to find gauzy crinoline drapery hanging all over the place to complete the Alhambra motif. I tried to see through it, but it was like looking through a fog. I pushed through until I saw the host's glittering jacket hanging on a hook. I knocked on the next door, then tried it. It was a feminine dressing room — with pink crinoline — and I was hoping at least to find Pretti there, if not Bunny herself. I waded through the harem decor until I got to a vanity, but there was no sign that anyone had been there lately.

At the next door, I heard whimpering, so I pushed it open, and was able to make out through the blue gauze the figure of a woman lying on the bed. "All right, Almond," I said, punching my way through the drapery, "you coward. What kind of a way is this to treat Bunny?"

No one answered, and I couldn't find Almond anywhere. But there on the bed lay Bunny beneath a blanket. Her hands and feet were bound to the bedposts by four small ropes.

"Bunny!" I yelled. Her eyes were open but still glazed over, her face now frozen in that stricken, tragic expression that was her trademark. I could see her with her high school lover in a faraway garden swing, her green eyes closed as she inhaled the night air. She moaned a little, then whimpered again. "Bunny," I said, "for God's sake — *Penny!*"

She did not so much as look over at me. I snapped my fingers in her ear, and they were smart little snaps, too, if I do say so myself — adrenaline snaps — but they did not register. Her eyes were ocean green in the blue haze of the room. I looked all around me for something to hit Almond with in case he caught me in there.

"Bunny, key out, for Christ's sake. *Key out!*" I looked straight into her eyes and for the first time she seemed to look back at mine. "Bunny, please, let's get out of here, OK? We'll go back to my hotel room and call the police."

I pulled back the covers. Bunny was wearing nothing but her bra and panties. What a sight she was, too, with her pale skin and beautiful shape, her black hair fanned out like a blackbird's wings on the pillow. I felt a stirring in me that bordered on the criminal. I doused the fiery urge and stood back to imagine her in the frame of a camera. How lifeless she appeared, like a mermaid I'd dragged up from the seaweed and laid here behind hanging webs of crinoline.

I reached down to cover her again, but as I did, I felt a hand on the back of my neck, eerie and electrical, and I recoiled. It was Bunny's cool hand. "Was it good, Franky," she whispered. "Did you enjoy it?"

"For Christ's sake, Bunny, get a hold of yourself," I said and took her by the shoulders and shook her a good one.

She closed her eyes. "Oh, Franky," she sighed as I released her, then sat beside her on the bed and looked into her glowing face. "I need you."

"I need you, too," I whispered, overcome with emotion. My mouth was an inch from hers. She smelled of vanilla. "How I could steal you away right now," I whispered, "and never bring you back? Where could I take you? I'd make us an Aeolian harp and find us a place where the woods and wind themselves would accompany those good songs you sing. We could forget about all the 290 million years that have passed and whatever days we had left if only. . . ." I felt her soft breath on my lips, and I kissed her. It was a kiss to last a lifetime, a Grecian urn kiss, an Orpheus and Eurydice kiss, Tristan and Isolde — pick a legend — Frank and Bunny. All I needed now was for Desmond Pencil to charge in to seal our fate.

I'd just caught sight of Bunny's dress lying on a plush blue chair beside the bed when I heard voices in the corridor. I pulled the covers back over Bunny, untied one of the ropes from the bedpost and crouched behind the chair.

I could hear an army of people enter, whispering. My heart thrummed like a hummingbird's. I heard a honk — was it a goose? — a bagpipe? — then the clinking of a glass or bottle — "It's the wee lass from the show," one of them said. It was the 48th Highlanders, for Christ's sake!

"Look!" I said and jumped out, startling the whole troop. "Look what Almond's done to Bunny."

"Ay, and a bonnie lass she as," one said. "As she all rright?"

"Yeah, I think she is," I said, "but what are you people doing here, anyway?"

98

Robert said, "Ay, well, we were wendering if Mr. Almond could carry on his wee show in one of our rrooooms, perhaps."

"You want him to continue the show. Listen, people, folks, whatever." I clapped my hands together and blew over the tops of my fingers. "I need your help here — look, the girl's tied to the goddamn bedposts. Something *bad* is about to happen. This is not a nice fellow who did this. If you have him up to your room, he'll have you dancing out of your window one at a time like the Pied Piper until you're all splattered on the ground below." The highlanders looked at one another. "I'm from Canada," I said — "John A. Macdonald, the Queen Mother, the Commonwealth — we're practically brothers and sisters here." I took one of the women by the hand and led her to Bunny. "Can you help me dress her?"

"Of course I can," she said as she sat on the bed beside Bunny. She untied Bunny's other hand which fell limp to the bed then leaned closer to her. "Come on, lass," the woman said softly.

"I can't seem to snap her out of it either," I said as I crouched over Bunny. "Key *out*," I said. "See? Key *in*."

I felt a gust of wind behind me and turned to see Robert in another handstand, his kilt around his chin, his wee bagpipe flouncing about again. Everyone laughed. The other bagpipes honked.

"Key *out*," I yelled at Robert and snapped my fingers at the same time.

Robert reversed himself, but his kilt was caught in his collar. He was beginning to sport another boner, too, so I helped him to straighten himself out amidst titters and guffaws. "What do you think this is here, Robby," I said, "some kind of nudist colony?"

"I'm sorry," he said and stepped back. "Trrooly."

"You want this Almond to continue your party for you," I said to him, "but you think he's turning you into an Olympic athlete, and you're going to wind up a porno star — don't you get it?"

"Trrooly," he said, "I'm sorry."

Bunny was now on her feet by the bed with her blue dress on. The lass who'd dressed her found one of Bunny's shoes, and I found the other by the chair I'd been hiding behind.

We heard some more voices now in the corridor, and all of us stood silent. The corridor, too, went silent. Then Almond and the glittering host burst through the door. "What's going on here?" Almond wanted to know.

I slung my arm around Bunny and hustled her toward the door. Almond blocked my way. The glittering host stepped aside. I pumped up steam and lined Almond up in my sights. I let go of Bunny and threw Almond one of the best Canadian body checks in my repertory, but the little man stood like a hunk of steel, and my shoulder and ribs hurt, to boot. Almond took a hold of Bunny's hand but was mobbed by the highlanders and hustled toward the bed. As I resumed my exit with Bunny, I caught a glimpse over my shoulder of the host. He was wearing his glittering jacket again, but his pants were pulled down, and he was being tied to the bedposts. I flew out of the room with my sleepwalking companion. Even at the end of the hall, I could hear crashes and honks from inside the dressing room as if Almond was being attacked by a flock of geese.

Though she wouldn't talk to me, I managed to get Bunny all the way down the mile-long corridors upstairs to the lobby. I sat her down near the good-natured doorman, waved enthusiastically in his direction and got down on my knees to whisper to Bunny: "You stay right here till I get back." She looked me straight in the eyes — a thrilling, jaded, zombie look — "No," I said. "On second thought, come with me."

I threw my jacket over Bunny's shoulders, then my arm and led her out into the night. I had to turn the both of us around to wave at the doorman who I knew was still smiling away at us and saluting. Somehow, I got Bunny up to our room, helped her out of my jacket and tucked her into my bed. "I'll be back in a few minutes," I told her and left *The Red Badge of Courage* beside her on the blanket. Bunny's riveting jungle eyes fluttered closed.

When the elevator door opened on the lobby, Pretti brushed past me and stepped in as if we'd never met. I thought, "Screw her," and headed back over to the Taj Mahal. I didn't want to leave the highlanders holding the bag, so I jogged through the happy Taj Mahal door and straight over to the concierge to ask him to call security. When I explained the situation — not as coherently as I would have liked — the same idiotic camel-look that Clyde got came over the concierge's face. I put the phone receiver in his hand, said, "Red alert — potential homicide here," and took off down the runway to the stairs.

I made it into Almond's dressing room to the back of the crowd of highlanders. "Loook, it's our Commonwealth friend," Robert said as he gripped Almond's hands and shoulders behind. Almond looked a bit shopworn, but there was no sign of serious damage. A second burly highlander now clamped the hypnotist around the ankles while a third unbuckled his belt and yanked his pants down around his ankles. "Key an," Robert droned into the back of Almond's ear. "Key oot, key an, key oot."

The host lay unconscious and glittering on the bed. Two more highlanders hoisted up their bagpipes and blasted out "Scotland, the Brave," while the troop marched in a circle around Almond.

There was little more I could do, so I shook a couple of hands as the folks circled past me and then retreated. The woman who'd helped with Bunny winked at me, as did Robert, so I winked back several times, saluted and took off.

I got to the tiny, cheerful admiral at the exit and, as he held the door open again, he said, "Hello, sir," as if I were going out for a late night stroll. This time I really would have hugged him and swung him around — he was that cheerful — but I was in a rush to get back to my own hotel.

A damp wind was coming off the ocean, carrying a saltwater taffy breeze, and I paused on the Boardwalk to zip up my reversible jacket. I imagined myself up in our room, calming Bunny, bringing her down from her flight around the galaxy, holding her hand in mine and reading a chapter or two from *The Red Badge of Courage*. I wondered what Clyde would think.

At the Resorts I said hello to our bigger, glummer doorman who ignored me and got right down to the business of opening the door for me, sensing possibly that I was feeling faint again and not wanting to detain me. I whooshed right up to the room and was about to open the door when I heard a woman calling out from inside. I couldn't tell for a moment whether or not it was a call of distress, and thoughts of Almond — or maybe even security guards from the Taj Mahal — rushed through my head before I realized that none of them had any way of knowing where I'd hidden Bunny.

The voice rang out again. I looked at my key and then the number on the door. I took a deep breath to get myself ready to burst through, but first I pressed my ear to the door. "Oh, my God!" the woman was yelling. It sounded like Bunny. "God, yes, oh that feels so good!" Was it Bunny? There was a tremendous thumping noise. Who else? "Yes, Bob, yes!"

Given my track record with Alice Harron, it was only then that I recognized what was going on. I listened again to the thumping, then slumped down the wall beside the door and began to sob in earnest.

Chapter Seven

I sat on the Boardwalk steps next to the old Steel Pier with my feet in the sand and my jacket zipped to the top, blue side out. The damp breeze now carried with it a light drizzle, and the ocean water heaved and swelled before me. A dim moon shone on the water, turning it into an old party dress with sequins. I was unaccountably reassured in the dark that a few surgical instruments and plastic bags were not going to cramp the ocean's style. It could toss back anything we threw its way and then some.

A great heaviness sat across my chest. I wanted to plunge into that cold sea or, at the very least, howl at the heavens. But I am not, by nature, a cold-sea-plunger or a heaven-howler.

Oh, what was I to do now — *what?* Why had I ever let myself get talked into coming down here with Clyde? Why had he even asked me? So I could witness him carrying on with his sexual conquests? How could I ever have been so stupid as to fall for someone who — *at best* — would choose me third after, one, Clyde, a married guy, and, two, Franky, an *imaginary* guy — and who knows who else? For all I knew, I was flattering myself. Maybe third place was occupied by a cartoon character — Spiderman, possibly, or Jughead. Maybe I stood fiftieth.

It is true Bunny was not mine to lose. If anything, she probably felt more attached to Clyde than anyone else at the moment. What was it about the guy? Could people not see that his every move was governed by those twin spheres he dangled in his pants, those small mythic orbs behind which he strolled into lounges and set his upper twin orbs upon a girl singing a few songs, and he was off to the races? Yet it was in the ferment of his actions that magic happened. I would not have been the one to pluck Bunny from that lounge of hers in Toronto, then look her up down here. Clyde had done it all, and I had skulked around hoping to gather up some of the spoils.

But had I not given Bunny pause that first night? Had she not lain down in an embarrassed sleep when she might have been anticipating a wild orgy with *Bob*? Had I not unconsciously represented a modest alternative to her? Why not? Was it not possible that at least one drop of the old Mayflower blood might flow through the veins of a single human being — even here in Atlantic City, the old faded jewel by the sea?

Maybe this place had just gotten off on the wrong foot. It was, after all, a culture that had piled itself up too high and so had so much further to fall. Where were Rudy Valee and his Connecticut Yankees when we needed them? What happened to Captain John Lake Young's grand Ocean Pier, the "Home of the Cakewalk," where Sarah Bernhardt made her first Atlantic City appearance? Where was his Million Dollar Pier, where Harry Houdini once appeared, then disappeared, where Teddy Roosevelt launched a presidential campaign, where the very first Miss America contestants paraded their wares? Where was Captain

Young's palatial house, Number One Atlantic Ocean? Where were the Gypsies to foretell the fall of their comrades? What happened to the Steeplechase, presided over by its monstrous Chesterfield Cigarettes sign with its twenty-seven thousand light bulbs, "the largest electric sign in the world"? Where was the Planters Peanuts store where they roasted peanuts fresh daily? Where were the human cannonballs and those Steel Pier Diving Horses who plunged with their lunatic riders into a small pool? Where were grand old Haddon Hall and the Chalfonte "Between the Piers"? Where was Marilyn, riding down this very walk on the back hood of the Grand Marshal's car? Did she have to lie down and die so unceremoniously in sympathy with the city and its doomed wooden promenade? Where did Merv hang out these days? Did he think smiling cardboard stand-ins were good enough? Where were the best, the worst, the loveliest, the biggest, the smallest, the tallest, the shortest, the oldest, the strongest, the liveliest, the deadest, the grandest, the peanutiest, the richest, the poorest and the happiest? Where had the party marched off to? What happens when a country packs up its shrill optimism and moves it out of town?

The last time I could remember feeling this way was the night I got the call from Alice Harron to tell me to hit the road because the Bible had told her so. It had been the right thing to do, as I've already said, but it still broke me up, and so at the time I'd taken my things — a change of clothing, a sandwich, my toothbrush and two Oh Henry bars I'd stashed in my desk drawer — stuffed them in a bag, walked right by my parents, who were playing bridge in the living room with the couple from next door, and headed out into the night. My mother followed me to the sidewalk before she asked where I was going.

"I just need to clear up a few things for myself."

"Are you sure you're going to be all right?" she said. She stood with her arms crossed and rubbed her upper arms.

She wore one of those knowing looks at the beginning of a smile — but serious all the same. It was a look I hated at times like these. She asked when I was coming back.

"Maybe never."

"All right," she'd said. "But please don't forget us."

"What do you think I am, an imbecile?" I said and darted off down the street toward the park.

My mother tells the story to this day and adds that I did not come home until morning, which is true, technically — it was 3:00 a.m. — and she and her friends still get a laugh out of it. I hate the laughs even more than the knowing look, but at least she had the sense that night not to chase after me down the street in the car and make an unnecessary scene, so I had to hand it to her.

My mother had always been sensible in that way. In fact, she was the one who had bought me the reversible jacket which now beat off the wind and cold. She'd given it to me on my nineteenth birthday — the night Clyde surprised me with the car. I resented the jacket at first because she and my father had never broken the habit of buying me useful, boyhood things, like lunch boxes and pants with elasticized waists. They would never have bought Clyde such things, not since he was ten, because he was more volatile and would blow up at them if they weren't careful. From as far back as I could remember, they always tried harder and tread more lightly with Clyde. I was the child they relied on to understand and keep my mouth shut. I was the one they asked to drop in on Glad and Sad, and I was the one they wanted sipping NyQuil with them because Clyde might have said something which would have set them off for a year, or he wouldn't have showed up in the first place.

The very night they gave me the reversible jacket was the night of my nineteenth birthday. I arrived at their place — I'd moved out after I'd landed the job at the camera store — before Clyde and his family did. I found my mother fixing Clyde's favorite meal, veal goulash with dumplings, instead of beef stroganoff, which was my favorite meal. I wasn't so sure Clyde would even show up — he sometimes wandered off somewhere after work and forgot himself — so I was especially hurt when I caught her in the kitchen stirring up the goulash.

"Happy birthday, dear," she said as she kissed and hugged me.

I tried to play it cool, not hugging back. "So what is this?" I said, lifting the various pot lids. "What are we having?"

She explained that she had unfairly prepared Jane's favorite meal, steak teriyaki, on my father's birthday and Jeffy's favorite meal, tuna casserole, on Clyde's birthday and was now trying to make amends.

"But Clyde was in Las Vegas on his birthday, and we celebrated it without him," I reminded her. "It would have been foolish to fix Clyde's favorite meal while he was sitting thousands of miles away, tossing poker chips and dice. And, besides, if you keep doing that," I said, lifting the last pot lid to make sure she wasn't pulling my leg, "you'll never make the right person's favorite meal on the right occasion, and you'll spend a lifetime revolving through the wrong meals on the right occasions just to atone."

She stopped stirring for a moment. "You're right, sweetheart. Do you mind, then, if we skip you altogether this once just to catch up?"

I stood there and shook my head. There she was, serving up meals like a baseball pitcher, hoping I'd swing through them — connecting only once in three tries. She got out from under my stare and dashed out to the front closet to bring me my jacket.

"Try it on. I know it will be perfect for you when you ride around on your bike. It's reversible."

"What does its being reversible have to do with me riding my bike?" I snapped as I checked through what I had to admit was a pretty clever jacket. The inner blue side had the exact same pockets as the tan side, and the zipper had a double tab, one inside, one out. "Do you mean I can't wear the same color on the outside day after day when I ride my bike or that I can't just *walk* someplace with the jacket on?"

Sometimes my parents seemed so out of it with their reversible jackets and their solutions to life's little dilemmas. I was suddenly overcome with a sadness I couldn't explain. I looked at my mother's face and realized she was hurt, so I kissed her. But I had to straighten up in a hurry because Clyde, Jane and Jeffy burst through the door just then, and Clyde was liable to have his first big guffaw of the evening at my expense.

Anyway, dinner did turn out all right because my mother had made me her famous chocolate cake and because Jeffy asked to sit beside me and kept hugging me practically every time he filled up his mouth and took a break to chew. And, waiting until the very end of the meal, Jeffy broke the news to me about the car parked outside with a ribbon around it.

The wind had mysteriously died down now, but it was raining in earnest, the dark clouds in the night sky dangling strings of drops straight down and pocking the sand at my feet. I hoisted my collar up around my neck and fought off the feeling of being pulled down the drain where my hormones, which had failed to observe my passage into my twenties, thought I needed to be. They'd neglected to boil up when I was grinding myself into the mud like Alan Bates and being breasted all over the map, for God's sake, but here they were now, trying to suck me down a sewer. I felt old and even a little arthritic, possibly.

What was it about Clyde's view of the world in general and about women in particular that I could not understand? I mean, I honestly couldn't have explained his position if I had to. If women, to him, were just a warm, soft place to nestle for the night, why couldn't Jane be as warm and soft as Bunny, or anyone else? What was the big difference?

Even more mysterious, what was it about Clyde that drew women to him? It couldn't just have been his whipped Elvis hair. Was it that he was so sure of himself and knew where he was headed every minute of the day? Was it that quality that enabled him to scare off guys at blackjack tables who made faces at his kid brother? Maybe it was his particular brand of bravery or maybe just foolhardiness, something he may have picked up from Kung

Fu movies, but whatever it was it impressed women, men and children alike. Even if they hadn't seen him in action, they seemed to sense that, when it came down to the crunch, he could turn to scruffy men with cigar ash dribbling down their fronts and tell them to get lost. He had the wolf's ferocity and the wolf's respect, too.

I remember once, not long after Clyde had bought me that Oldsmobile, I went over to his place to give Jeffy a ride. Clyde was reading the paper in the living room, and Jeffy banged on the back of the paper and said, "Dad, do you believe in God?"

Without even looking out from behind his paper, Clyde said, "No." Just like that.

Jeffy looked at the back of the paper for a few seconds, shaping some of the words with his mouth, then asked me if I wanted to see Ricky, his hamster. Up in his room, Jeffy shook Ricky's tiny plastic house inside his cage so violently that I thought he was going to shake the poor little bastard's organs loose. The hamster came out — maybe he'd gotten used to that kind of shaking — yawned and stretched as wide and long as if he'd been on a rack. Then Jeffy said to me, "Do you believe in God, Uncle Eddie?"

I pondered the question for a while before answering. "Jeffy, did you see the way that little hamster stretched and yawned?"

"Yeah?"

"Well, that's exactly the way we stretch and yawn. It's hard to believe it was just by accident that we do it the same way — that we went our separate ways for millions of years, hamsters and us, and just stumbled on the same way to yawn by accident. Do you know what I mean?"

"Not really," he said.

"Well, have you ever seen a peacock, the way it prances around? Have you ever seen the way it spreads out those long, colorful feathers? I mean, have you ever seen anything so ridiculous in your life? Nothing happens that way by accident. The peacock's someone's idea of a joke. It's a kind of thing for poets and such to pick up on and compare foolish, prancing people to and for the pharaoh's slaves to fan the pharaoh with. Or look at a giraffe with its leopard spots and horse's body and those little wick-like antlers at the end of a mile of neck. Have you ever seen one of those things standing in a zoo? What kind of fool animal is that to have standing in a zoo? Am I making myself any clearer?"

"Not really," he said.

"I mean, it seems part of some grand design, in this case someone's idea of a joke. Look at a peach. It's sweet and juicy and delicious, but look at the outside. It's like biting into a sweater. Am I getting through to you now?"

"A little," he said.

"And the *irony*," I added — "the irony is that we've screwed up the natural order of things, we humans. Look at cats. Do you know what cat food is made of? It's made of horse meat. We have cats eating horses — do you know what I mean?"

Jeffy yawned wider than Ricky and asked if we could take the ride in the car.

It was not until that very moment, as I recalled the incident, that it occurred to me that Clyde's answer was a better one to give, in a way — better for a father. It really *didn't* matter what Clyde's opinion was — Jeffy would decide for himself sooner or later. What mattered was the definitiveness of the answer, the absoluteness of it. Clyde had given the answer of a father, and I'd given the answer of an uncle. If Clyde was going to be an atheist, everyone would know about it. He was the type who'd have a Jewish family over for dinner and serve roast suckling pig, then stare them down, waiting for a challenge. Maybe that's strong, but not too strong.

With the rain coming down on my head and nowhere for me to go really, I felt right then like stealing Clyde's car and doing some damage to it — not serious damage, mind you, maybe just a little nick or two — but damage all the same, something that would take him out of his way to an auto body palace in the neighborhood. Or, better still, I felt like throwing his cassette of *My Fair Lady* out the window and running over it a couple of times. What would the Great Bob of Atlantica say then?

And then something miraculous happened. Just as I was pulling up my jacket over my head to make a small tent out of it, a couple of Canada Geese strolled by me in the rain, stopping on their way south and foraging around, probably, for some washed-up fish. I felt tears coming on again and wished I had something I could toss their way, a crust of bread, anything, to reassure them they had a comrade here. I thought of Henry Fleming going off to get his *Red Badge*, and how his mother had packed him a jar of blackberry jam and eight pairs of socks which she wanted him to send back for darning just as soon as they developed holes in them.

I wanted more than anything to talk to someone about the geese. I wanted to say how regal they looked, how the seagulls for yards around cleared out of the way just as soon as the geese swooped in. I wanted to rush up to the Taj Mahal and tell the little doorman what I'd seen in the rain, and what a boost it had given me. I'm sure he would have cheered me on even if I'd walked through the door as he held it open for me and walked right back out again.

But I couldn't go near there just now on the off-chance I'd run into Almond. Maybe I could have a short chat with my own grim doorman, and maybe gladden his heart. I could ask him how he became a doorman. Did he like the job? — did he view it as a kind of craft? — did doors appeal to him at an early age? — but I would have risked having the whole thing blow up in my face, especially if he backed into the job after a life of broken dreams which had started out with him playing with fire helmets and stethoscopes.

I resolved simply to take a ride somewhere. I still had Clyde's car keys in my pocket and could drive off to Amish country in Pennsylvania for all it mattered, and I'm sure it would have been Thursday before Clyde noticed I was missing. I tried to pet one of the geese on the head before I left, but it scampered away from me toward its mate, scattering the gulls still wider.

Chapter Eight

When I got back to our bright hotel, I barely said hello to our doorman, and that suited him just fine. I walked past him to the garage without going up again to check for thumping sounds coming from our room, then drove off into the rainy night. The truth was I didn't know where I was headed. All I really wanted to do was get out from among the palaces.

I had this vague notion as I passed a phone booth to pull over and give Pretti Tangerine a call at the hotel to see if she wanted to go out for a drink or some coffee, or even just to ask her what had happened with Bunny and find out if she'd had the same experience when she got up on stage with Almond the night before. But I was worried she'd brush me off, and I didn't know if my ego could have withstood another blow that night, so I drove on.

My legs and feet were wet, and I felt a chill judder over me even with the heating on full blast. In no time I was out of shouting range of the casinos in a part of the city where the Boardwalk narrowed. I doubled back and looked for some place to dry off and warm up with a drink. But there were no lights to be seen, none in the windows of the old houses, none in the closed-down shops with their ancient, faded lettering over the doors — the Milliner's, Samuel's

Haberdashery, The Atlantic Fish and Chip Company, Since 1896. Eighteen ninety-six to what, I wondered. These places should have posted the year of their demise up there as well, like the years on gravestones.

I drove a while longer until I reached a dark district beside what looked like a canal, but it might not have been. I was hoping to find a doughnut shop open. There was something eternal about a doughnut shop; all other shops could sputter and die, but as long as there were truckers and traveling salesmen and nighthawks, there would always be a need for a place which served hot coffee and sweet doughnuts. But here there were none.

Up ahead, through the whipping windshield wipers, I could see Oriental Avenue and the neon sign of Barclay's Saloon flicker on and off. It was the first sign of life I'd seen, and I thought I'd give the place a try. There might even be a hand dryer in the bathroom I could use to dry out my running shoes with.

There were only a couple of cars in the parking lot when I pulled up. But I found I had to brace myself before going in. I wished I had someone with me — not for protection, nothing like that — just someone I could walk through the door with and continue a conversation with as if we'd been having it all day. I would have been proud even to have had a couple of highlanders with me. Anyone. Even Jeffy — especially Jeffy — or because it might be too late for Jeffy, Bunny. I would have given anything to talk over some things about books and music with her, have her tell me how she'd gotten started with Ray Charles's music. What was the very first song of his she'd learned and sung along to? Did she think she ever wanted to give a real concert somewhere? Had she ever sung on a street corner, and was that where her manager had found her? Did he do something cool like drop a business card in her guitar case instead of some loose change? No, I decided, not that guy — not a guy who makes her sing a medley of all of Western music before she can squeeze in a song or two by Ray Charles. What I would have given to have had Bunny with me with her shiny black fusilli hair and simple blue dress. But who was it — *who?* — who'd rescued her from one wolf's den and allowed her to stroll off right into another one?

I stared through my weeping windshield at the warm glow streaming out from Barclay's windows like the orange glow in a watercolor. I ran in through the rain and pushed open a big, old, steel door with a few dents in it — I was glad there weren't swinging half-doors the way there would have been in a mall back home. I was glad, too, to see an old wooden bar and a worn, planked floor that sagged in the middle. The place had a jukebox and pool table at one end and a dart board in the middle with five darts crammed into the bull's eye. It was smoky and ragged but bright. If it had been in one of the hotels or in that mall back home, it would have had pictures up of Billy the Kid, and maybe a saddle or two on the walls, but this saloon, smack-dab in the middle of the ghost town section of Atlantic City, had the look of a place visited by real modern-day desperadoes and gunslingers, people who might have sold cocaine rather than the deeds to land with gold in the ground. The only thing missing was the actual desperadoes.

There were only three customers in all: a young woman sitting at the bar, eating chicken wings and drinking a Coke and a large guy with a kid not much older than Jeffy at one of the round tables. The bartender was a tough, middle-aged woman who looked as if she'd seen a few things and probably had a rifle stashed under the counter. I wondered if she was any relation to Barclay. She eyed me up and down as I took a seat a few down from the chicken wing girl and scanned the menu which hung above the bar.

"Do you have hot chocolate and cinnamon danishes?" I asked.

"No, we don't," the bartender said. She was wiping the counter in front of me. The place was overheated, but I felt grateful for it. I looked up at the meal card again. Under the "Beverages" section, it said "Fruit in Season."

I didn't want to blow it again since the entire bar had come to a standstill since I'd walked in, so I whispered, "Do you have apples?"

"Yep, I think we do."

"OK, good. I'll have an apple, and do you have anything hot? I need a hot drink. Do you have Viennese coffee?"

The woman looked at me. "We have Irish coffee."

"Perfect," I said. The woman went out to the kitchen. I wondered how long it would be before this place's neon sign sputtered out forever, but I had a vague feeling it had staying power. It was only Monday after all. On the weekends, I was sure there were dart tournaments and dancing and a good deal of shuffling back and forth between tables in search of cheerful cocaine customers.

I turned to peek at the big guy and his son. They weren't talking, but they were both busy fiddling with the salt and pepper shakers and other loose objects on their table and seemed quite happy to be doing so. The man was smoking, too, and had a beer in front of him, and the boy had a half-eaten order of French fries with gravy shoved off to the side.

While I waited for my coffee, the girl at the bar spoke to me. "You're not from this area?"

"Me? No. How'd you know?"

"I haven't seen you here before."

"Oh." I thought she was going to say it was my accent. "I'm from Canada," I told her, then for some reason added, "We have different money up there."

"Oh, cool," she said, not about the money, I was sure. "You came all the way down here to get in some poker and stuff? Are you staying at one of the bed and breakfast places down the street?"

"Bed and breakfast places? I didn't see any of those."

"Oh, yeah. They've been restoring a few of these old places like crazy lately, not two blocks away."

"Oh, really. I didn't see them." The girl was quite attractive when you took a close look at her. She had pretty brown eyes and dark blond hair, though it is true the hair was a bit too long and bushy for her narrow face, and there was too much blush on her cheeks which was meant, I think, to make her look robust but instead came off making her look a little feverish. But the big drawback with her was that she had a raspy voice — as if the dial hadn't been set quite right on her voice — and people with sore eyes or raspy voices make my eyes water for no reason I have ever been able to account for. An acquaintance of mine, a biology major, told me the problem was called empathy. All I know is that it was really quite embarrassing most of the time. If a friend or someone arrived at my place with a sore throat or red eyes, I'd start bawling right away. Not a burst dam kind of crying, but a mild tearing all the same. I once even had a vague chest pain which was hard to describe because it was definitely a chest pain, but it felt as if it were happening outside myself somewhere and was hovering over me in the room. The next day I found out I'd had a bit of somebody else's heart attack. We got a call from a hospital to say that my grandfather had been taken in with one.

Anyway, I was discreetly wiping one of my eyes when the girl told me her name was Brenda and added, "You have really nice dark red hair — unusual," as if there were no such thing in the United States.

"Oh, thank you. That's very nice of you to say." I introduced myself and thought right away of Alice Harron, and about how nice it would have been right then to lie down with someone in a warm, dry bed — just to have my arm around someone, mind you, nothing lewd, necessarily. But Brenda had not moved any closer to me at the bar and she had that raspy voice which made me cry. I would have to explain that sooner or later if we were going to share even a night together, and it would probably kill any chance of a relationship right on the spot. She would know right away that we couldn't spend time together if I was going to be weeping like a baby every time we discussed what movie to see or the price of a dozen eggs in New Jersey as compared to Ontario.

Besides, Brenda had pushed away her large plate of chicken wing bones, and they sat there on the plate beside her as if a whole flock of small birds had flown by and she'd snatched them out of the air like some Gila monster and polished them off down to their bones. She reminded me suddenly of this great aunt of mine who turned up one day at our place after she'd escaped from Russia with her son, and she started cooking chicken soups with the chicken's feet thrown in for flavor. That was fine, but she'd sit there at dinner and slurp on the boiled feet, getting right down there between the toes to suck the flesh right off them. And if you watched her too intently, she'd smile and say, "Congratulations," because that was the very first word she'd learned in English from cards we'd sent her in Russia, I guess, and she was proud of it. She'd walk right into our house, pinch our cheeks, Clyde's and mine, and say, "Congratulations, congratulations." We'd say, "Thank you," and congratulate her right back. Maybe I'm being harsh in my judgment — after all, my aunt's family was even still not out of that immigrant period when you wear bad clothing — but luckily, she'd moved away to Paramus, New Jersey, just up the highway a couple of hours from where I was now sitting.

I pushed these thoughts to the back of my mind as my Irish coffee and apple arrived. The apple came on a plate with a knife beside it. I guess the knife was there because the bartender might have sensed that I was getting on and was having trouble with my teeth. I moved down the counter one seat almost to within breasting range of the girl. I took off my damp jacket and placed it on the stool on the other side. It was then I noticed that Brenda had on a white skirt, white stockings and clumpy white sneakers. "What do you do?" I asked.

"I'm a nurse," she said, clearing her throat. So that was it — she might have picked up a germ in her throat at the hospital. Maybe she knew of something I could take for my watery eyes. Maybe she'd heard of the phenomenon. "I've just gotten off my shift," she said, "and thought I'd drop in here for some dinner."

"I didn't realize there was a hospital nearby — I didn't see one."

"Oh, yeah, there's a good one. I mean, it's not Camp Boardwalk or anything — "

"Camp *Boardwalk?*"

"Yep. Didn't you know that? Camp Boardwalk was the nickname for this place that was the biggest hospital in all of America, and it was right out there on the Boardwalk." Brenda's feverish face brightened with patriotic fervor. "That was during the last war; and all the soldiers were brought there for treatment."

"The soldiers? I didn't see anything out on the Board-walk."

"Oh, it's not there any more. It's been remade into a hotel now, I believe. It's called the Resorts."

"The *Resorts?*"

"Yeah, have you seen it?"

"I certainly have."

I wiped my eyes and tried my coffee. It was good and hot. I could feel the whiskey burn its way down my throat. I then cooled it off with a good loud chomp from the apple to prove my teeth were still in perfect working order. "Do you live in the neighborhood? I mean, it looks as if no one lives around here, except for those bed and breakfast places you mentioned. There are no lights on anywhere."

"Yeah, I know, it's sad." Brenda took a gulp of her beer. "But there are lots of people," she went on. "They're just squirrelled away in the houses around here. The places are kind of like tenement buildings. The people who live in them don't turn on lights because they don't want the police to clear them out. Actually, the police really couldn't be bothered with them much any more, but they don't seem to know that. They're always scared. I work near here, but I live pretty far away actually — well, maybe five miles, over in Ventnor — that's not so far by car, I guess. What about you? Are you here on your own just to do some gambling, or are you passing through?"

I noticed for the first time how full and red her lips were, even without lipstick, and I got a powerful urge to kiss her.

"No, I'm here with my brother Bob," I told her. "He's the big gambler, really. I'm just here to take in a couple of shows and get some reading done." My mind lighted on *Sticky Days in Tahiti* and suddenly it was *my* face that felt feverish, but Brenda smiled sweetly. I wanted to tell her about the Mike Almond show I'd seen and what had happened afterwards, but I was afraid it would upset her, and that was the last thing I wanted to do, especially now that I recalled her "nice dark red hair" remark. I pictured her checking in all these people without medical insurance in this old Victorian neighborhood, opening their children's mouths to have a look at their throats and taking swabs with those long Q-Tips, or rolling up the sleeve of some old daughter of runaway slaves and reading her blood pressure. Then I got to thinking how difficult it would be to relocate in Atlantic City with nothing but hypnotism shows and blackjack to go out to, and only *Cherry Blossom Gets Plucked* listed on the movie page. That's the kind of person I was. I hadn't even made it over to the stool next to Brenda yet, and I was already imagining the movie page in *The Press.*

I poured some sugar into my coffee before taking another sip and gave it a good long stir. The man and the boy behind us were getting set to leave, and I wondered whether the kid had school in the morning to go to or what the story was. Maybe they were just passing through, too, on their way to some ailing uncle in the Carolinas. I decided that was the way I wanted to leave it and not trouble myself with the boy's sleeping hours.

The bartender asked if I wanted anything else, and when I shook my head, took off for the kitchen again. She was probably a one-woman operation — on Monday nights at least.

Brenda, too, seemed to be wrapping things up, and now I could feel my pulse quicken as I searched for a way to invite myself over to her place. "What are you going to do now? I mean, do you go off home and get some sleep and do your shopping or whatever in the afternoon, before you head out to work?"

"Yes, that's about right, but I usually wake up before afternoon. I like to see whatever I can of the morning sun. Look," she said. She was rummaging about in her purse.

I wanted to spring the story on her suddenly of how some Highlanders and I shoved around Mike Almond to give me some of Clyde's wolfish quality, but I lost my nerve. When I saw Brenda taking out a pencil and a small piece of paper she'd torn off an envelope and writing her name and number on it, though, I blurted out, "Do you want to have a little dance maybe?"

It was the last thing in the world I wanted to do. I was a terrible dancer because, whenever I was out on the floor, I could never stop thinking about how goofy my body became with my arms pumping this way and my legs swinging that way with no particular place to go, so what I always did to intensify my goofiness was keep my head down so I could watch my own stupid body moving around with a mind of its own, just to make sure it wasn't getting tangled up in some way that I was not aware of.

Brenda handed me her number and said, "What — here?"

"Yes, here. That's all I was thinking." God forbid we should go out now to scout around for some dance palace. I'd meant one quarter, one goofy dance.

"Well, OK," she said, hesitantly.

"I wonder if they have any Bunny Tremaine numbers," I said as we walked to the jukebox.

"I don't know," Brenda said. "Is she Canadian?"

"No, she's a local — and an up-and-comer. You should watch out for her."

We danced to "Heartbreak Hotel" — or at least I did — I didn't have a chance to look up to see what Brenda was doing. And when it was over, I looked into her narrow face and said, "Well — "

"Well," she said, "do you think you'd like to come over for some hot chocolate? I have some at my place."

"Yeah, sure. Do you want to take just one car, or — "

"No, you can't leave your car here. It probably won't be here when you get back. Doesn't that kind of thing go on where you come from?"

"Oh, it does, but I come from a place where, if you're walking down the sidewalk and you turn and point your finger across the street, you can stop traffic. It's really amazing."

"Wow. Well, OK." She looked away for a second before saying, "Why don't you just follow me, then?"

I picked up my jacket and deftly reversed it in one move, practically, so that I could have the dry, tan side on the outside and sauntered toward the door with Brenda.

But as soon as I got to my car, I knew I was making a terrible mistake. What could I have been thinking? It wasn't the 2,500 chicken bones or anything — I doubt I'd looked so dainty and attractive myself, I'm sure, after I'd eaten my sardines and left their little zippers all over my plate. It wasn't even her voice. (I'd stopped dabbing my eyes, come to think of it, just as soon as I'd gotten used to listening to her.) It was something else. I was the kind of person who couldn't just lie down with someone in a warm dry bed, then scoot out of there and continue my life, keeping up the relationship with a quaint postcard or two flying between cities. I hated quaint postcard relationships. I hated even hearing about them or seeing them in movies. But that's how I was. I took one chomp out of a fruit of the season with someone and my imagination was already off somewhere having children with her. That was why I hadn't yet succeeded in finding a warm dry bed to my liking, not even with Alice Harron. Why couldn't I settle with quieting down my heaving hormones just this once and be done with it? Why did I have to watch myself every second the way I'd just done on the dance floor? The only person — and it did not dawn on me until that very moment — the one solitary female individual I thought I could forget myself with was Bunny, and what had I done with her? I'd left her in a daze to wail out "Bob!" into the night, and that, I was now sure, was as close as I would ever get to being with her in this lifetime.

My wipers were slapping the rain to one side and the other as I pulled out of the lot behind Brenda's small, white sportscar, a car she'd picked out, I suspected, to offset the clumpy white shoes she always had to wear. To my surprise, she had quite a lead foot on her inside that clumpy shoe, and I had to scoot right down those slick, dark Atlantic City streets to keep up with her. I had no idea where I was going, naturally, even if I could have slowed down to read the street signs, and when she'd put a block between us, then turned just where the road widened, I lost her.

For a moment, I thought I'd picked up the War Memorial out of the corner of my eye, but I couldn't be sure. I followed one of the bigger streets, thinking it was Atlantic Avenue, but it turned out to be Ventnor Avenue, and I saw a small sign which said, "Ventnor/Margate/Longport Next Left." I hung a left and, when I caught the familiar pair of pointy red lights turning in on Buffalo Avenue, I followed and was relieved to find I'd stumbled on Brenda's little white car again, just as it pulled into the driveway of a small, frame fourplex.

Chapter Nine

I deliberately clumped up the stairs behind Brenda, so she wouldn't feel embarrassed, but she turned to me in the dark and said, "Shh."

She let us in to a small but bright apartment, decorated with a great deal of netting, colorful navy flags and a model schooner perched on top of a small TV. "Make yourself comfortable," she said, indicating the couch. "I'll get the hot chocolate." She dropped her keys on the coffee table and slipped off her shoes beside me, so that I caught a glimpse of small, delicate feet, straining pinkly against those white stockings.

"Do you like seafaring paraphernalia?" I called out to the small kitchen. But she was not there any more; she'd slipped into the bedroom. I waited a while, took off my jacket and noticed a pen and a small pad of Post-Its with a phone number scrawled on the top sheet. Beside it sat an Atlantic City/Margate/Ventnor/Egg Harbor phone directory, and I was seized by a desire to look up Bunny. I flipped madly through the book and decided I'd say I was hunting for pizza places if I was caught. I didn't *want* to make an excuse, but it wouldn't hurt to have one standing by. There was no one listed under "Tremaine," so I tried Lopez and found, to my surprise, that there were a dozen of them in the small book but none under "P" or "Penny."

I wondered what Desmond Pencil, my talisman, would have to say about all of this — Bunny, Almond, Brenda, the whole bit — or rather what effect an early evening sighting of Desmond would have had. I noticed a steel cylinder propped up on a stand sitting like a trophy on Brenda's TV set.

How could I stay here? How could I drink a person's hot chocolate and then take off out of there, never to be seen or heard from again? How could I do this to Bunny? OK, so we weren't exactly the talk of the town, but if I ever got there — if I ever got my chance to tell her what had happened after I'd hustled her away from Almond's dressing room, how could I explain sharing someone else's hot chocolate and admiring her seafaring paraphernalia only a couple of hours after tucking Bunny into my own bed? Oh, what I would have done right then just to take a good, long look into those green eyes of hers!

Brenda was wearing a big, bulky bathrobe when she brought me my hot chocolate, and she had her hair pinned up away from her narrow, pretty face. She'd even wiped off that feverish blush of hers. She hadn't brought a cup out for herself, but she sat in a soft chair beside the couch and watched me as I took a sip.

"I like the ocean motif in here. It's very nice. Where'd you get that big fishing net over there on the wall?"

"All of that stuff belonged to my dad, actually," Brenda replied, the rasp in her voice worse than ever. "My grandfather was a cod fisherman up in Maine for many years, and my dad was in the navy during the war, so I guess I have the sea in my blood." My eyes were watering again.

I actually launched a tear right into my hot chocolate. "One of these days," she went on, "I think I'd like to take a trip around the world in one of those great big ocean liners."

"What about that thing there?" I was pointing to the metal cylinder atop her TV set.

"That's a metal cylinder."

"Oh," I said, and she smiled.

I put down my cup and gave my face a good rubdown. "What's the matter?" she said. "Do you have something in your eye?"

"Yes, I think I do."

"Ah, that's too bad." She got to her feet, and I thought she was going to examine my eyes, but instead she rasped, "Listen, do you mind if I have a quick shower?" There was a sultry little edge to the rasp now, too. She paused, pulled out the pins in her hair and looked over her shoulder, hiding out, almost, behind the hair.

And that was what did it for me. If she'd strolled over and had a peep at what was in my eye — even a disinterested little peep — she'd have tipped the balance, and I'd have dropped my damp clothes right there and then and followed her into the tub. In her situation, I'd have hauled out penlights, tweezers and Murine if I suspected that even a passing acquaintance had something caught in her eye, but Brenda passed me by without so much as a concerned furrowing of the brow.

"Go ahead," I said. "No rush."

"OK," she said. "Well, make yourself at home."

As soon as she was gone, I picked up the Post-It pad, folded over the phone number and began a note to her:

Dear Brenda,
    I know it could have been fun, but I have this condition of the eyes which I think you should know about. Also,

I tore out the sheet, taking the phone number she'd written with it, fastened the number down again, and started a new note:

Dear Brenda,
    You're a wonderful girl, but there is someone I haven't told you about. The other thing is that distant relationships

I pulled off that note, too, and crumpled it into my pocket with the other one. I started again and got as far as *"Dear Bre"* when I heard a noise in the bathroom, grabbed my jacket and scrambled out of there.

Outside, I had one last look up at the lights of Brenda's apartment, memorizing them for myself almost because I knew I would have no photograph of it. I felt the damp wind's chill, got into the car and drove off.

Chapter Ten

At the end of the road a couple of blocks from Brenda's place, I detected the swampy canal I thought I'd seen some time before, so I turned again and came to a stop at the corner of two narrow streets, just to take a breath.

Up ahead, in the fan of my headlights I could see four guys come walking out into the road. There were no lights on in any of the houses, and I found my knees were trembling as I moved forward and tried to navigate my way between the two of the guys who were now blocking my way. I didn't see any guns pointed at me, so theoretically I could have barreled right through, but the guys in front didn't look as if they were going to budge. Maybe these were the cocaine desperadoes on their way to Barclay's. I stopped and rolled down my window.

One of the guys wore a toque as tight as a condom on his head, but he was very polite. He opened the door for me with a grand sweeping gesture like a hotel valet and said, "Outta da cah, please."

I soon found out they all talked the same way. One of the guys had what looked at first like an egg growing out of the side of his forehead, but it was dark and shiny as if he'd been struck by a mallet. He listed a little as he ambled toward me and said, "Joo got any coin for us, my main?"

"Coin? No, I just used up my only quarter in a jukebox up the road a little ways."

They all found my answer quite witty, I think. The one who'd stood in front of the car at the outset I now noticed had a scar which ran diagonally across his face, as if someone had tried to cross it out. I took a mental note of this, in case I made it to the police and had to describe these guys. Adding him to the toque and the egghead, I gathered this was the Damaged Head Club. Except that the fourth guy had no visible deformity; he might just have been a damaged head trainee.

The crossed-out guy was smiling so broadly (if a little crookedly) at me that I believed I could have made friends with him under different circumstances and might even have swung him around together with my little doorman. The egg-headed guy, though, was clearly the leader (and might even have been "Taranchoola" in for a visit from Philadelphia). With a sweep of his head, he pointed with his egg at me, and, leaving the trainee behind, the smiling guy and the toque ambled toward me.

In my hurry to reverse my jacket when I'd left the bar with Brenda, I had forgotten to move my wallet to the inner pocket. Not that it would have made that much difference — but there it was — you could see it down there in my jacket without having to look, bulging away proudly like the leader's head. To my astonishment, it was actually my smiling friend who stepped up to me, got hold of the wallet and ripped it out, pocket and all, leaving a long flap of jacket dangling in the rain.

What I would have given just then for just one ounce of Clyde's wolfish nature. Clyde would have growled, his eyes would have widened with rage, he'd have puffed up his chest like Hercules, and he'd have gotten killed, I was sure, but he'd have gone down in flames.

That was not me. I just stood there, obediently following the eight-step guide put out by the P.T.A. on how to deal with these situations. And then I burst into tears, not with sound effects added — I managed to swallow the sobbing portion — but it was a good healthy flood of tears nonetheless. And to make matters worse, I thought I was going to wet myself both bottom and top, but I managed to suck it back in.

After the egghead had rifled through my wallet and found nothing more than about forty U.S. dollars and ten Canadian, and no credit cards whatsoever, he didn't look happy. "What da hell is dis?" he asked, pulling out the purple Canadian note and holding up Sir John A. Macdonald's face for the others to see. He muttered something in Spanish to his pals — something disparaging, I was fairly confident — then listed toward me. He saw that it was not rain that was streaming down my face, jammed the bill way down in the flap of my jacket behind my pants belt and gave me a little slap on the wet cheek. He asked, "Joo have the tine, main?"

"The *tine?*"

I rolled up my sleeve, and in one nifty motion he snatched my Underwater Timex right off my wrist and into his pocket. "I'll need dis for furder reference," he said.

I stepped back and tried with all my might to cough and swallow to steady the quiver in my voice before saying, "Well, OK, thank you very much."

"Fuggin' guy," the toque snorted.

I was shoved to one side, and the four of them scrambled into the car, two of them huddling in the cramped space behind the front seat. I stood watching them, relieved, if you can believe it, and practically waved, for Christ's sake, as they pulled away. They drove half a block, then screeched to a stop. The crossed-out guy rolled down the window on the passenger's side, yelled, "What the fugg is dis?" He threw several cassettes into the road, and then they drove off again, crunching the cassettes beneath the Allanté's tires. I followed them up the road, saw that *My Fair Lady* had been spared, and put the cassette in my side pocket.

And all I could think of off the top was what Clyde would say about losing *Oklahoma* and *Guys and Dolls*, and I felt deeply sorry about it.

And why hadn't those guys dropped me off somewhere at least — somewhere near a bus stop or a doughnut shop? It was true they could have dumped me in the ocean among the syringes and bits of intravenous tubing, but what kind of hell-hole place was I standing in now?

And then, my very next thought — and this is the kind of guy I am — I should strangle myself one of these days — my Number Three thought was what poor Brenda was going to think. She was going to come out of the bedroom freshly showered and in a negligée, know that I'd had a change of heart, that I'd taken a look at her clumpy white shoes on the dance floor and her pretty face which might have narrowed more than it should have, studied the naval paraphernalia one last time and taken off. Not that she'd slowed down much to see how I was doing when she was leading me to her place. Maybe she'd also had a change of heart after Barclay's and had tried unsuccessfully to lose me up these alleys and streets. Who knows? When someone's supposed to follow *me*, I drive like a snail, pulling over past a red light if that person didn't make it across in time, and then getting out and flailing like a lunatic to make sure the individual knows I'm still there. But then I come from a place where you can point a finger and stop traffic. I'm sure it's the most civilized place on earth — not that that doesn't have its drawbacks. And if Brenda was trying to lose me, why had she given me her phone number and later sashayed off to the showers? She must have been sincere when she did that. By now, she must have gotten out of her bedroom in her negligée, saw my "Dear Bre" note, looked sadly at her fallen shoes by the coffee table, then wandered over to her box of hot chocolate powder and wondered where I'd gotten to — maybe even sat by the phone for a minute or two before going off to bed because she knew I had her number, had taken off, but could still use it to make arrangements for brunch.

I began to feel sobby again — began, in fact, to feel I might topple over onto my stomach right there and bawl like a baby. I needed to find a phone fast and was glad to see one just up ahead on the corner of what turned out to be a main street, called V-something, probably Ventnor, but I couldn't be sure because the rest of the sign had been chopped off by someone. Across the street was a church no bigger than a cottage, called "The Way of Life Assembly of God Church," a real mouthful but I guess it had to be for such a small church.

The V-something street sign looked positively unharmed compared to the phone. Crumbs of black plastic on the floor were all that were left of it. The lower metal panels of the booth itself were pushed in on all sides and two of the windows had dried vomit sprayed all over them. The metal cord of the phone dangled pathetically. I took it in my hand and examined it to check the ends of the little colored wires poking out of it — and for what purpose? What was I going to do — *repair* it? I swear, I involve myself in some of the most useless activities on the globe, and half the time I'm not even aware that I'm doing them.

I turned to look out of the phone booth at two pairs of sneakers bobbing on the frayed telephone wires above. The lights were out in all of the houses behind me, but it must have been after 3:00 a.m., so they should have been.

It was only then that it hit me: Thought Number Twenty-Two. I had lost something important tonight besides Brenda and *Guys and Dolls* — had *known* it was missing, in fact, somewhere in the back of my mind — otherwise, what would I be doing, standing here in a barfy phone booth gawking at two pairs of executed sneakers? My brother's car. Oh, God, what was I going to tell Clyde about his car? That four guys, three of them with damaged heads, had simply swept it out from under me? That they'd *asked* me to pull over on some crummy street and, though I could see no deadly weapon, I'd happily obliged them by handing over the keys and wishing them a safe drive? And what had they used to threaten me? Maybe they'd been disciples of that comedian with nothing but his box of bullets back at the Taj Mahal. I could explain to Clyde that they were mean-looking and that, even if they hadn't bothered to show me their guns or knives, they must have known their way around their neighborhood deadly weapon store. How else would they have gotten their faces crossed out or grown a second head?

Clyde would have to know how I'd felt. He'd even been best *friends* with someone like these guys, a guy named Hank Abbott, whose father had been sent to prison for killing someone in a brawl and whose mother drank away her afternoons. Hank was the first high school student in the history of Harbord Collegiate to have taken on the sadistic Mr. Winslow, the chemistry teacher, who used to punch people right out of their chairs when they were fooling around. When Winslow walked down the aisle toward Hank one day, after Hank had been trying to get my brother's attention across the room, Hank had stood up, caught the teacher's flying fist, slammed it down on the desktop, then lifted Winslow up by the collar and hurled him across the chemistry counter at the front and into a huge mound of beakers and Bunsen burners. Winslow stood up, brushed the 2 million bits of glass off his jacket sleeves and out of his hair, and said, "That'll be all for today." That was Hank's last day of school ever and, even later, when he'd moved on to a career of fire-bombing beauty parlors and crossing the border with mysterious parcels, Clyde kept up his friendship with him and helped him out of some difficult scrapes by calling lawyer friends.

Clyde knew these types of guys. Would he have expected me to take on someone like Hank if he'd commandeered the car I was driving down some dark street — let alone three guys like Hank and a trainee?

I was sure Clyde could get back both the cost of the car *and* the deductible, anyway, because Clyde had insurance friends to go along with his lawyer friends, not to mention police friends to round out the circle. I'll never forget the day, not long after Clyde had bought me the Oldsmobile Calais for my birthday, he wanted to take me to the horse races because I'd never been and he said I didn't know what I was missing. (I *did* have an inkling of what I was missing and didn't want to go, but what could I say after he'd bought me an Oldsmobile for my birthday? I'd, after all, gotten him a brown vest for his.) We were driving along merrily when Clyde told me to step on it — "see what this baby can do." I'd gotten the baby up to 80 in a 40-zone when I heard a siren behind me.

I pulled over, the cop got out, sauntered toward my window and said, "Are you Edie?"

"No, the license bureau ran out of Eddies, so —"

But then he saw Clyde. "Hey, Markson," he said, "how they hangin'?"

"Great, just great, buddy. Hey, Jackson, listen, this is my kid brother."

"Not another word," Jackson said, holding up his police hand. "Just cool it out here, will you?"

"No problem. Thanks, man." And off we went. Now, what were the odds of that happening, I ask you?

If Clyde had ever been held up, chances were it would be by friends, and they'd send him on his way with a slap on the roof.

But I was not Clyde, and I was sure he would understand just as long as I told him how terrific he'd have been in the situation, whether it'd been Hank who held him up or Taranchoola himself. Clyde always went in for compliments like that and would forgive anything when he got them.

No, I could never be Clyde. I could eventually develop into someone like Dr. Rinjert, that insane ear, nose and throat fellow who wanders through casinos and grabs people's heads to examine their ears, but Clyde: never.

I would have to get to a phone now to call the police just as soon as I'd gotten through calling Brenda to explain my sudden departure, and Clyde — but not until after the rain stopped — and not until I'd gotten through relieving myself behind the barf booth — which I needed to do even before the rain stopped.

I stepped out, scurried behind the booth and launched an arc that would have made Clyde proud. A powerful tremor whinnied down my spine and, just for a moment, as I stirred the fleshy puddles of Atlantic City, I felt more satisfied than I could remember. I felt like Stephen Dedalus, pasting his snot on a rock.

And then, feeling the cool rain on my back, I returned to my booth, and with a shudder began sobbing like a damaged hyena.

Chapter Eleven

Sometimes I get a yearning, but the yearning has no shape or, worse, no locale — like an internal itch. And yet the yearning is no less intense for its not having a shape or location. It makes me want to fly a plane to Peru. It makes me want to ride the surf or scale tall buildings. But I am not a rider of surfs — or *surves* — or a scaler of buildings. I am a snapper of pictures and a drinker of coffee, and an eater of danishes whose yearnings rumble through me and explode without a sound.

Maybe such yearnings stem from the fact that I've always been the nice guy. If one of my pals was in trouble, I was the one who hung back and listened after everyone left — not because I wanted to but because I had to.

Once when I was 17, my friends and I went out to play late-night hockey in my best friend Sid's father's Lincoln. The car was all of one week old. We jammed into the Lincoln, six of us, played the beautiful stereo, set the Climate Control Center on blast and headed for the arena. On the way, though, someone knocked the flame off Bruce Bush's cigarette, and it fell between his legs onto the upholstery. He jammed it out with his finger, even spit into the little burn hole, and for good measure, once we'd arrived, stuffed snow into the hole. While we were playing hockey, though, we heard sirens screaming outside. At the time, we thought nothing of it.

But after the game, we shuffled out of the arena just in time to see firepeople rip the last of the smoldering seats out of the car. The interior of the Lincoln was gutted and black. Even the steering wheel buckled like a blob of chewed black licorice.

The guys slipped away and took the bus while Sid and I stood by to answer questions. They then went off — the firefighters and police — to make calls and fill in reports. Sid asked me to drive the car home with him.

"What are you talking about?" I said. "There's hardly anything left of it."

"There's nothing left of the interior, but I bet it still works."

And so we did. Though the police had warned us to stay away from the car, we crawled into the tar can, I sat down on my hockey bag, and Sid on one knee worked the melted pedals all the way back to his place. The car even had a nice kind of zip to it with the load off.

When we got to Sid's place, his parents were already asleep. "Will you come into their bedroom with me?"

"I don't know, Sid."

"I can't do this alone."

"What do you want to do?" I said. "Don't you think it might be easier to kill them in their sleep than tell them what happened?" Sid thought about that for a second. "Come on," I said.

So we went, and in the darkness of Sid's parents' bedroom I stood trembling as I heard Sid whisper, "Dad, we burned down your car."

"What, Sidney?" he grumbled.

"The car. It's had a bit of a burn."

I'll never forget standing outside in the driveway as Sid sobbed, and his father looked through what was once the window of his new Lincoln. I stood there like a bloody saint, then sat with Sid for another two hours before heading out into the night on foot for home.

The truth was I did not have the courage *not* to be a nice guy. I was not brave enough, like other guys, to say no when I felt like it, to push people off. People said I was terrific — a great, great guy — but really it was a matter of courage, of slipping away from the rink with my guilt and heading home to put the guilt to sleep.

So I was the guy people called, and I was the guy who went, even when I truly didn't feel like it. If my parents were flying off to Florida or Costa Rica or wherever-the-hell place, they'd call me to take them to the airport. No big deal. The salient point, though, is that they would *never* call Clyde. The last time they asked, Clyde told them to take a limousine and he would foot the tab. And I was the one always snapping the pictures of the parents waving good-bye as they headed through the airport security equipment "because you're so gifted with that camera of yours, sweetheart." And I was the one waving hello through the quarantine glass in the baggage terminal as they returned home with their tans and their sombreros. For my efforts, I too was rewarded with a sombrero and a small, plastic guitar.

And I was the one my mother called when she took ill with that mysterious parasite she brought back from the Caribbean. She thought for a long time that it was the flu, and I did some shopping for her while my father was out of town. "Look at me, I'm feverish," she said, gasping for air. "Feel my neck, how sweaty I am," she said. "I'm drenched." For the record, I do not like to touch people's sweat, but I did so to humor her.

The interesting result of these efforts was that I did not earn extra credits in the love department. On the contrary, I was the one whose favorite meal could be skipped over on my birthday because I would understand, the extra effort of sweat-touching having faded from the record.

So maybe that's why I get these powerful yearnings: because what I was really good at was flapping like laundry on other people's lines.

Whatever happened to Marvin Gardens and the Community Chest and the Reading Railroad? Where was the little mustachioed man with the cane and top hat? Where was the iron thimble? Had people forgotten the glittering diamond ring with its luxury tax of $75.00? Where had Camp Boardwalk gotten to? Where were Bert Parks and Bob Barker? Was the Miss America Beauty Pageant not held here each and every year? In what fancy little nook did they tuck those beauties? What cheerful red bus were they hanging from — smiling and waving — and to what crowds? And where was the bus going? Did it lurch down these crumbling streets with their ragged gardens and back lanes suffocated with garbage? Or was that the Miss Universe Pageant and San Francisco? Where was Walker Evans now with his camera?

I sometimes wish that I could have been an explorer — I would love to have been the guy who first set eyes on this jewel by the Atlantic. I can only imagine what it would have been like — like being the first person to stumble on Niagara Falls — hearing the roar from the distance, pummeling through the bush — then — oh! I can imagine what it must have been like to have been Paul Gaugin, slipping out of his family house in Paris, sailing away to Tahiti, anonymously penning *Sticky Days in Tahiti* on breaks from his painting. But this town was a place long past exploring, the buildings burned out from above people's heads, the floors sagged out from beneath their feet, people living alongside the ghosts who had moved in. Like Tahiti. Like Niagara Falls. Once you point out the roaring miracle, then people move in and put up their own sad miracles: neon signs proclaiming Wilf's Fried Chicken — 24 Hours. Rainbow lights beamed out onto the falls. Wax museums — when all the famous people in the world, past and present, cannot help you celebrate your wonder of the world, they can do so in wax, I guess.

And so I stood in my phone booth, pressed against the disgusting glass, waiting for what? Waiting for a cheerful red bus full of Miss America hopefuls to come by to pick me up? Come to think of it, I hadn't seen any real buses in Atlantic City since I'd been here, just the little chopped-off jobs, called Jitneys, which came by only once in a while and not at all at this hour.

I turned in the booth toward the darkness behind me. Maybe this is where Bunny had come from, one of these bent little crates of houses. I had not even asked her, before marching her off to our room at the Resorts, if she was from here or how I could get her home. Oh, what I would have given at that moment just to be able to ask Bunny if she'd grown up in one of these houses and to say I understood how her name had come to be Bunny, to say those chunky palaces on the Boardwalk must have seemed pretty special from her angle and that she'd made quite a leap for herself, getting started in a career singing in one of their rooms, even if it was only medleys. I wanted to see her now just for a minute, to imagine her face from the sound of her voice on the phone and to tell her what I thought of these things. It had been so long since I'd met someone I could talk to, and Bunny seemed just the sort who'd give me that minute or two. That's what she had become for me: someone to talk to — or not necessarily talk to even — maybe just another heartbeat in the room.

Oh, stupid, greasy, mealy-mouthed, dick-directed, Kung-fu-fighting Bobclyde! How could you have yanked the one true love of my life out from under me — overcome her as she lay in a trance in our room and planked her before she knew what'd hit her? But then how could you have known, you Elvisian moron, that she was my love — or even that it was your tiny dear brother who had rescued her — and for what? — to serve Bob's greasy little needs.

I put my hand out of the booth to test for rain, then looked out and up at the sky and took a deep breath. Once, when I was half as old as now (or maybe it was a quarter), we visited Saskatchewan because my father said that we had to do it once in our lives. It took days and days to get there, and on the way we passed through and stopped at towns with streets about as long as pantlegs. When we finally arrived in Saskatchewan, my father pulled over at a spot where there were no houses, no lampposts, no *trees* even.

"What's this?" Clyde had asked, but our parents were already out of the car. "Watch," Clyde said, "he probably has to take another leak. Do you need to take a leak?" he asked me. "Because if you do, I'll have you a contest to see who can piss the farthest."

"No, I'm ok right now," I told him. If the world were run by Clyde, we'd all be in tournaments day and night to see who sprinted the fastest; who took the shortest time to write a memo; who snored the loudest; who spent the fewest hours getting the highest marks; who bled the most through the nose; who could keep a ball in the air with a paddle the highest number of times; and who pissed the farthest.

We got out and looked, but nothing happened. Our parents stared at us like monkeys.

After two or three minutes of this, Clyde broke the silence: "Can someone tell me, please, why we have stopped here in Nothing, Saskatchewan?"

And then it hit us — hit even Clyde who never went in for these things. What there was was field and sky — the widest country, the biggest green field and fattest blue sky anywhere on the face of the earth. The kind of place that really made you want to get naked and grind yourself into the earth or turn over on your back and gape at the fat blue dome.

And where I stood now, a half or three-quarters of a life later, was the puniest place: a narrow phone booth, the tiny Way of Life Assembly of God Church across the road and, when I looked up, the thinnest shards of purple sky you would ever see. And what excuse did anyone have for it, for putting up these piles of stone and peeling planks to huddle against the vast Atlantic Ocean — for *naming* their city after it, for God's sake, then cutting up the sky into splinters?

The rain had turned to mist. I stepped out, slung my wet jacket with its hanging flap over my shoulder, felt another shiver judder down my spine and headed out. I saw a gang of boys approach from down the street. I saw them sling a beer bottle out into the road where it smashed, and I darted across the road to the little church.

I was suddenly terrified that this new pack of wolves had seen me and would rip me to pieces. I waded through a deep puddle to get around to the back of the building and, to my surprise, the door was slightly ajar. Just as I reached for the handle, a small, dark figure opened the door and stepped out. "Oohh!" I leapt a yard backward. There stood an old black woman in a rain coat and a plastic bonnet. "What are you doing here?" I asked.

"I couldn't sleep, so I went into the choich to pray fo' my Sander."

"Sander? Oh, I'm so sorry. Excuse me."

The woman adjusted her white hair beneath the bonnet, fastened the tab at her neck, then trudged off down a small, dark street behind the church. She was wearing a man's big boots and seemed to be wading around in them.

The inside of the church was as modest as the outside. There were plain wooden pews, a wooden cross up front and a simple glass candelabra, sitting on a table covered by a red, velvet cloth. This particular night, it shared the tabletop with a single, lighted memorial candle in a glass which cast a small yellow apron around itself. It had probably been left by the poor little woman who couldn't sleep.

Though the church was quite cool and damp, the candle made it seem a little warmer.

I chose a pew in the second row, the floor creaking beneath my feet as I crossed the aisle, and took a seat.

I have never had much rapport with God, mostly because I was never quite sure what to say when I faced Him, so I ended up staying quiet. But even in a place as unimposing as this one, I felt the need to spout something weighty, particularly after God had heard about Sander and the life that woman must have led since he passed on, trudging around on a wet night, wearing her husband's big boots. I knew God had a sense of humor — what with the peacock and giraffe, not to mention Jeffy's hamster who'd gone his own way for six billion years and still stretched and yawned the way we did. Still, I wanted to avoid uttering something silly like "I am an eater of garlic bread," or some other such thing that customarily entered my mind on these occasions. I gathered most people asked for things, like the worshipper ahead of me on this night, but I couldn't think even what to ask for. You can't amble into a church and ask for your Allanté back or your brother's *Guys and Dolls* tape, even if you manage to slip it in during a long stream of devout-sounding babble. I didn't want to ask for a safe return to the hotel either because, carless, walletless and Underwater Timexless as I was, I was no longer much use to anyone, and I was fairly sure I'd make it back before the week was out.

What I wanted to ask for, badly, was Bunny. I wanted to ask the Lord to give some thought to how we'd work out as a couple. Possibly, He could send Desmond Pencil by to give me a sign. But if it worked — if Bunny were to fall head over heels for me, if we were to make mad love and have five children together — somewhere in the back of my mind, I would always wonder if she really meant it or if she was just *made* to mean it. If Mike Almond could make Bunny swoon, surely the creator of the universe could whip up a little razzmatazz. It isn't even that I'm a devout person. If I'd read in the morning paper in the horoscopes that someone was going to fall for me that day, and then Bunny came along and leapt into my arms, I would wonder then, too. But I didn't want to ask for something corny — like good health for my parents or a fine education for Jeffy — so I was left with very few options. I thought for a moment I might ask for Brenda to forget she'd ever met me — which she might have done already without my having to ask — but just in case. Even if I'd managed to get in touch with her again some time that night, I would still have to come clean and tell her it wouldn't work out with that raspy voice of hers and that feverish face and me bawling all over the movie pages. Finally, I just got to my feet and creaked out toward the door. No wonder people took up speaking in tongues. They must have been like me: they couldn't communicate with their Maker, so they decided they'd confuse Him instead by yammering like banshees.

Just as I was about to leave, I stumbled over someone lying by the door and shouted out with fright. My first thought was that it was a corpse, but the body groaned when I kicked it. I was ready to bolt out of there, but decided to look the guy over first before I did. I rushed to get the candle left for Sander and set it on the arm of a pew near the guy. He was groggy and dressed in what must have started out as a spiffy three-piece suit but had now turned shabby with dirt, stains and what looked like tire marks across one arm. He had a tie poking out of his jacket pocket like a marsupial. His hair was gray, and still looked combed, but he had thick, black eyebrows like insects lounging above his eyes. The man sat half-way up when I realized he was holding an ashtray.

"What are you doing here?" I asked.

"I'm resting," the man said. "I've been staying here the past couple of nights. Would you care for a smoke?" He held up a half-crumpled pack of Lucky Strikes. I took one and realized that some of the tobacco had fallen out of the end, so that when he lit it, the end flared up and startled me. The guy held up the ashtray for both of us.

"What's with the ashtray?" I asked.

"It's a gift for my girlfriend." The bronze ashtray had the Taj Mahal molded into its base. The man hoisted himself up to an erect sitting position, his black caterpillar eyebrows arcing with the effort.

"I took a few bucks from my bank account back in Milwaukee — the truth is I inherited a few bucks from an uncle — not much, but still a few happy bucks — and I thought I'd have a little break from this work I've been doing at this trucking firm — I'm Assistant Manager, Accounts, there — no big deal, but it's not a bad job. So she goes — my girlfriend does — 'Don't gamble away your life savings, Ted, I'm begging you,' Joanne says, and she even gets down on her bloody knees, which really pisses me off because we've *been* to Atlantic City together, and she even told me the first night that her shoulder ached from yanking the slot handles all day long. So I remind her that it's just like that here. It's an all-or-nothing, do-or-die place. There aren't many like them — New York, maybe, at night, but hardly any other place. It's all or nothing, like you could lose your last two hundred dollars or make a hundred and sixty-five thousand — that's possible, too. There is no middle here — like middle America and middle age. The middle world got squashed out into the two ends with everything at one end and nothing at the other. All the glamour and entertainment right out on the end of one of those piers, or the same pier gets blown away in a hurricane and what's left of the party has to go home. You get all the wealth of the baccarat, or you get to lie down on one of those sewer grates for some warmth for the night. That's the excitement of this place. And Joanne knows this — she knows it about Atlantic City and she knows it about New York. That's the east coast for her, and she says she's never coming back."

"Why not?" I asked. "Because of the money you lost?"

"No, it was something else — the weirdest, stupidest thing," he went on. "Totally out of left field. It was New York we were in on our second anniversary — kind of our second anniversary — because we're not really married or even living together, but the second anniversary of our dating, and we were in this restaurant near the Ed Sullivan Theater. It was real nice, and we were feeling mellow because we'd just taken this romantic ride on one of those horse-drawn buggies through Central Park. Anyway, we're having our meal, real gentle and romantic when in walks this crew from David Letterman's show. They were playing 'If We Pick You, You Can Come Eat Your Meal Right on Stage,' or whatever the damn game is called —

and it wasn't even late night like everyone thinks, but late *afternoon*, actually. Anyway, this crew goes to one table, camera and all, and there's this older lady in a hat, eating some fish and chips, and we hear Letterman's voice over the sound equipment, interviewing the woman live on the show, asking her where she's from, where she got her hat, that kind of thing — totally out of left field as I say. Anyway, Letterman, he goes to her, 'You're not very interesting,' because he's not really talking to her but *through* her at America, and suddenly the crew is coming toward us, and Joanne grabs her purse and is madly brushing her hair, and Letterman himself suddenly asks Joanne where *she's* from, and she goes, 'Billings, Montana, originally, but now I live in —' but he interrupts her, see, and says, 'Ma'am, what's with the brush?' She's forgotten she's still brushing her hair and looks like someone hit her over the head with a brick. 'It's not your hair,' Dave goes, 'that's going to get you in here to have your meal with us.' Then he asks her what she does, and Joanne seizes up — she can't say a word — and he says, 'Well, aren't you a fascinating pair,' or something to that effect, and we can hear the studio audience laughing, and the camera swoops away from us. I'm watching all these other people after that, watching where the camera's going, and people are trying to be funny and clever, and I hear Dave's voice saying, 'Isn't there anyone interesting in that restaurant, there, Bill?' and they go to a commercial while Dave's scouts scurry around like mice, trying to find someone."

Ted unsheathed another Lucky Strike and swallowed dryly.

"So what happened?" I asked.

"So I look over at Joanne, and she's crying — bawling

her eyes out, as a matter of fact — and the trip is ruined. I knew it that second. You couldn't have felt sorrier for anyone in your whole life than I did for Joanne at that moment. Things couldn't have been worse after that. We flew back west two days early. There's a point, when people are trying to be funny — and it doesn't work, or at least not for everyone — when comedy becomes mean. Do you know what I'm talking about?"

I nodded.

"And maybe it's because she knew this, that fun sometimes turns bad, that she goes, 'Don't go again, Teddy. Don't go out east. It's our little nest egg you'll be losing.' So I tell her, 'What if I bring back a whole dozen eggs — extra large — instead of just this one?' She just shook her head, no, and took off. I left her a message on her answering machine that I loved her, I needed a break, I'd be back soon, and I'd even bring her a present." The guy let out a raspy breath. "So I got her this ashtray," Ted said, his voice trailing off. I dropped my butt in beside his. Ted's face looked, in Sander's candlelight, like a campfire face telling tall tales. The light bobbed over his smiling, purple eyes.

"Why don't you go back home, then? Is there any way for you to get home?"

Ted lit his second Lucky Strike, the end flaring up. "I had to cash in my return ticket, and it wasn't much. It was just a bus ticket. I called Joanne to give me a hand, told her to wire me some money at this particular bank, but she wouldn't. I can't say I blame her." Ted dropped an ash in the ashtray.

"Look," I said, "why don't you take this?" I pulled out my only money.

"Look at that pretty thing. What's that?"

"It's ten dollars, Canadian."

He took it into his hand to examine it, turning it over and over. "Why do you have Marty Feldman on your ten-dollar bill?" he asked.

"That's not Marty Feldman — it's John A. Macdonald, our first Prime Minister."

"That's so cool. And it's purple, holy crow. It's like Monopoly money. Listen," he said, "why don't you keep it? It's OK. I'll try to call my brother in Toledo in the morning, collect, see what he can rustle up for me."

"I'd give you something else — or I could probably help you out a bit myself in the morning — but I was mugged tonight."

"Oh, that explains your jacket," he said, giving the torn flap a tug. "It's a rough place, that's for sure, or it can be, boy-oh-boy. But no, thanks. You've been nice enough already, sitting here listening to me ramble on about Joanne and Letterman and whatever. I think I'll call my brother, as I say, or maybe even my boss back home — he's a good head — comes here himself when he has a chance, or to Vegas. Thanks, though, anyway."

Ted offered me his hand, and I shook it and felt better than I had all night — almost as good, in fact, as when Bunny asked me that first morning about what people see in reading.

But when I got outside the church, I suddenly felt sorrier than I ever could, wondering how many people might be skulking around little church corners, holding ashtrays. I wondered too, again, if I would have left Joanne back home and come out to Atlantic City this way with my savings.

The gang of beer-bottle hurlers was long gone, and I crossed back over the street and walked down one block, then broke into a run until I reached the canal at the end. I didn't know where I was anymore in relation to the hotels nor even whether I was heading back in the direction of Barclay's, a place I would have given anything at that moment to find again. I knew, too, that if I was to so much as head up the walk of any one of the tiny houses on the street behind me and peer in the window, I might be greeted with a shotgun blast before I'd made it around to the door to knock.

On the corner up ahead, I could make out two dark figures, sitting, facing the canal. They might as easily have been bushes as people; still I crept my way along to find out. I darted to the opposite side of the street as I drew closer, so I could take a cautionary look. They were certainly people, but they were still as stone as they sat together. I jogged over to them and made a faint throat-clearing noise. Neither of the bums budged. I drew still closer and could detect one of them bobbing gently. I coughed again, putting my hand up to my mouth so they wouldn't think I was trying to spread germs.

"Excuse me," I said. "Would you mind telling me the way back to the Boardwalk down near the hotels."

One of the dark forms turned out to be a woman. She looked at me, and even in the dim light I could see crystal blue eyes gazing out of a dark, unwashed, round face.

I said, "Do you happen to know the way to the Resorts?"

The man beside her got on all fours in an attempt to get to his feet. He was even dingier than his partner. I wondered how long they'd been sitting there, watching the canal water glub by. The woman continued to stare at me, not saying anything, her eyes fixed on me. I held out my ten-dollar bill, and she looked at it, then back at my face.

Then, to my surprise, the man made it to his feet and started pointing behind me. "You go on down to Ventnor behind you whey dey's a little choich," he said, then listed before steadying himself. "You move on down to da lef' whey dey's some big steel bins dey use to put out da gahbage dat da trucks pick up mornings, a blue bin an' a great big yellah bin; you go along pass a Mini-Mart wit' da bent bahs on da windah, close' now dis time ah night, cut right trough da motahcycle lot dere nex' to da fillin' station, left trough da noisery school lot ovah da ole wooden fencet, den da steel fencet, whey dey's a ben' in the fencet so's you doan need tah cut youah fingahs climbin', run on down trough da lane but watch some ah dem boys sometimes lookin' fah a bit of fun, trough dis ole apple orchahd with dah little gnarly trees, an' you'll get round dah fron' ah a empty buildin' was once a glove fact'ry ovah towahd dah place across wit' da iron chaihs on da verandah, pass dah hydran', a yellah one, if I'm not mistaken, Isabel, towahd da ole commahce point, right pass da Mobil fillin' station, pass a phone boot', a broken lamppos', pass da little wooden house — guy use' to sell 'em fron' ah da salt watah taffy folks out dere on dah eastehn en' ah da Boahdwalk, still do, oh his son do, I'm not shoah which — whadda ya know, Isabel? — takes you leftwahd towahd a dock trown up on da greasy sand one day in a stoahm, I believe, heading down den no moah den a hunerd yahds to dah beach dis en' ah da Boahdwalk."

"Well, thank you very much," I said, ready to break into tears, just as a single quack of laughter burst from my throat, a damaged hyena quack. I had to turn away and convert the noise into a fit of coughing as the guy made his way downward on all fours again to take his seat beside his partner. I was still holding up the ten dollars, but neither of the two seemed too moved by the gesture. I offered them the *My Fair Lady* cassette but still couldn't get a rise out of them. "Thanks again," I said.

I was once in Rome and standing by some great fountain when a good-natured lady who'd seen me studying a map came up to me and spent ten minutes telling me, in Italian, the way to Hotel Cinquante — or Something-Cinquante. For all I know, she might even have been a fortune teller, telling me I had 50 days left to live — that's how much of the conversation I'd understood. I stood and smiled through the whole ordeal, then walked off politely to where the woman had last pointed as she smiled and egged me on. This is the way I felt right now. I was ready to die of embarrassment at the thought that this helpful guy here had heard my short blast of laughter. But he gave no sign he had and waved at me as I trudged away.

I remembered, at least, to go on down to Ventnor again and turn left. Then, suddenly, way up ahead of me I saw the headlights of a car turn down the street toward me. Was it Brenda? Had she given my disappearance a second thought, sensed that I was not the type to take off the way I did, remembered my dark red hair and given the streets one last scuttle before retiring?

No, it wasn't. It was a cab! I pulled on my jacket to give myself more of a packaged appearance, ran down the block, leapt out into the road and flailed like someone on a one-tree island. The cab roared up beside me, splashing the hell out of me, and I darted around to the driver's side, holding up my jacket flap with one hand and giving my splashed pants a wipe with the other. The driver was a tiny, haggard man with milky brown eyes and with one of those German sailor caps the Beatles wore in their German sailor period.

"I'm off for the night," the guy said.

"I can't tell you how sorry I am to hear that," I said, "because I need a ride just up to the hotels — to the Resorts," I tossed in to give me more authority. "Can you just go that far?"

"I'm off for the night," he said again in his dry, haggard way.

"I know, but you see I'm a bit stranded here and don't even know where the hell I am, and I —"

I felt tears coming on and swallowed hard. I looked into the back at his dry, warm car seat. The driver craned his neck out the window behind me as though I had someone lurking in the bushes ready to spring and said, still looking back, "Payment in advance."

"Oh, OK, do you accept Canadian funds?"

"No, cash only, in advance."

"Well, you know, in some places Canadian funds are thought to be cash —" He'd already begun to roll up his window. "Listen, please, I was mugged just a while ago back there, and my car was swiped right out from under me. I'm staying at the Resorts, I swear, with my brother who's a huge international investment broker, and I'm —" The window was now completely closed, but he hadn't driven away yet — "I'm in the film industry — I've made some very big pictures."

The window stayed up. The driver adjusted the bill of his cap, not that it helped him in any way. I was holding my ten-dollar bill up against the glass. "It's not Marty Feldman," I said. "Look around the eyes."

"Payment in advance," he mouthed at me, "twenty bucks, Canadian." He held up the fingers of both hands twice.

"How about Barclay's Saloon? Can you at least get me there?"

"Better stand clear," he shouted. And he checked over his right shoulder to pull away. I stood back a few inches.

"Can you tell me which way to walk, for Christ's sake? *Which way?*" I shouted. I was pointing both ways when my jacket flap became unhinged again and curled pathetically down my thigh. But the cabbie was gone in a flash, and when he was, I remembered I was alone in the street and might have caused quite a ruckus, so I beat it out of there in the opposite direction of the cab. I darted along for several blocks and had to slow down to catch my breath, but the run made me feel warmer and more assured. After all, I was still alive if a little damp, and how long more would I have to lug myself around one street and dash up another before morning came and the Brendas and bed-and-breakfast guests of the world would be out again in their cars, going this way and that. I could flag one down, then, for sure, and be on my way.

If only the cabbie had told me which way to go, I would have felt altogether well and quite tidy. Or even if he'd said he was off for the night and that was that but given me a minute to sit in his cab and talk to him about this place — ask him if he'd seen the Mike Almond show or heard Bunny Tremaine sing or sat on the Boardwalk and watched Canada Geese stroll by, or been to Saskatchewan to see the sky there or talked to the nice little doorman at the Taj Mahal or caught David Letterman once in a while. I would even have let him listen to *My Fair Lady* during our talk. But instead the guy gave me the leper treatment right off the top and then swooped away. That was what didn't sit right with me.

It was at that moment I looked up and saw lights blazing from the windows of a house a block and a half away. I ran toward it as if I were running home. As I approached, I could see that, though it was the same size as its neighbors, the house looked neater and had a late model black Lincoln parked in the driveway. I could see inside through the big picture window that there were all kinds of people milling around, men and women both, as if it were the supper hour, and I could make out music — "Old Man River" from *Show Boat* — playing on a phonograph in an old stereo.

I reversed my jacket again, turning the torn flap-side in, strolled up the walk, pursed my lips for no good reason I could come up with, except maybe to whistle, and tapped lightly on the door.

Chapter Twelve

No one answered, so I banged with my fist. A small man in a black suit opened the door and said, "Come in," as if I'd been expected.

I stepped forward and beheld a man three times the size of the first, dressed in a T-shirt with a belly like Buddha, sitting on the couch, presiding over the room. "Come in," he said, "come in. You're just in time for Ezio of Cabrizzi with the pants. He should be by any minute — fact, I thought you might be him."

"No, I'm not. I'm Eddie of Canada."

"Just as good. Come in, take a load off."

I was wondering now if the night really hadn't taken its toll and I hadn't wandered into a mirage. Maybe they thought I was Clyde, or someone like him, I mean. The place had a carnival air about it, and I guessed everyone was welcome and everyone was waiting, probably for this Ezio, who must have been special in some way. There was an oldish woman dressed in a mini-skirt and gold blouse, smoking a cigarette and sitting in a chair beside the couch. Her hair was dyed and coiffed, golden and big, like a retired Grand Ole Opry singer's, and she had surprisingly shapely legs for an older woman. Still they were a bit too pale and veiny for a mini-skirt. Maybe if she'd gotten some color in her legs. I accepted a Camel cigarette from her and learned within two minutes that she'd been a Radio City Music Hall Rockette at one time, which would have explained all that fuss over the legs. She got up to switch off *Show Boat*, just as Paul Robeson boomed out his last, "*Ole Man Rivah, he just keeps a-rollin' aloooong!*"

Then she returned to her spot beside me. "I'm not from there," she said, as if Radio City were a state. "I'm originally from Indianapolis."

"That's great," I said.

The small man in the black suit who'd answered the door sat beside the ex-Rockette. He was twiddling a string of worry beads. It turned out — and if I'd been given 50 guesses I'd have gotten it wrong — he was a retired pawnbroker. I pulled off my jacket, taking care to hide the flap inside, and sat in the vacant chair between the two of them.

I asked the man, "Is there much call for a pawnbroker here in Atlantic City?" and won over the whole room with laughter.

He waited for everyone to settle down. "I owned a shop just up from the Boardwalk," he said, "called Cash for Gold. Do you get my drift?" And then there was quite a bit more guffawing and chuckling. I knew right away that Clyde would never have tripped up on that one. He might even have known a couple of pawnbrokers and might have whipped up some small talk on the spot and have made himself right at home.

A pretty black woman, dressed only in a slip, was standing in the kitchen doorway and talking on the phone. A girl of ten, possibly, also dressed in a slip, who could easily have been the daughter of the woman on the phone was in the corridor with her back to me most of the time, tossing horseshoes at a peg at the other end of the corridor, except it wasn't horseshoes she was tossing but hair bands. I wondered whether there were any schools in Atlantic City, or whether there was some strange breed of nocturnal child who lived here but nowhere else on the planet.

"I once owned a gas station just up the road from Vegas on the way to L.A.," the retired pawnbroker said. He was now spinning his worry beads in the air like a majorette. "These people would drop in on the way home from Vegas and want gas. Do you follow my drift?"

"So far, yes," I said.

"I'd be filling their tanks, and they'd stick their heads out the window and tell me they were a little strapped for cash — would I take something as collateral till they got home to L.A. and came back to pay me? 'Like what?' I'd ask them. 'Like the spare tire I got in my trunk,' they'd say — 'brand new, *mag*.' I'll tell you, I got anything and everything: Rolexes, wedding rings a lot of the time, Armani suit jackets right off people's backs — you name it. I even had to build a big shed out back to store the stuff. One guy even wanted to leave me his little kid — just to prove he'd be back by the end of the day with the money for the gas. Course, I didn't want no little kid and believed he might *not* be back to get 'im. That's how sorry the place was. So when I heard they were building casinos here in 'Lannic City, I asked myself, 'Why bother with gas?' — do you follow me?"

I nodded as I searched for a little clearing in the huge, bronze ashtray beside me to squash out my Camel, which had gone straight to my head, and turned, finally, toward the most striking figure by far: the big man on the couch, waiting for Ezio. He looked exactly like a large, white version of Louis Armstrong. He had about 400 teeth, the same jowly cheeks, smiled like the Cheshire Cat and even held a handkerchief by his side on the couch. The only thing missing was the trumpet.

"Do you know what I've learned in life?" the Louis Armstrong stand-in said to me. He was pouring himself some bourbon out of a bottle on the table in front of him. "I've learned two things: that you can't love anybody too much, and you can't pay anybody too much. Does that sit right with you?"

"It sure does," I said. "It makes a lot of sense." I was nodding in agreement, but no one else seemed to be paying attention. Maybe they'd been tossed these pearls before, or by the looks of them maybe they had enough pearls already for a few necklaces.

Satchmo opened his great, bullfrog mouth and flushed his whole drink down his throat. He said, "Yep," mostly to himself, then wiped his mouth with the handkerchief. "Oh, and one other thing," he said, leaning forward. "There are plenty of guys more sleazy than a used car salesman, and do you know who one of them is?"

"No, I don't," I said.

"One of them is a used-car customer."

"A customer?"

"That's right."

"How's that?" I asked.

"He tries to outsmart the salesman," Louis said. "He makes an appointment, and he doesn't keep it. Do you know how often that happens — that he makes an appointment and doesn't keep it and doesn't call?"

I shook my head. "My daddy was a used car salesman," he said. "He had a very hard life — that much I know. But it also depends on your take on things, I know that, too."

"Just how do you mean?" I asked him. I was having the time of my life.

Louis leaned forward against his girth, his brown eyes aflame, and said, "It doesn't matter what you believe in as long as it's *something*. Then, even if everyone else in the world thinks you're a sorry sight, it won't matter to you — you'll be glad about yourself because you'll be doing what you believe in.

"What I mean is that to understand people, you got to wrap your eyes around things. You have to look at things from different angles. If you look at an apartment building from a long ways off, it's like a big, square ant colony, but you go inside one of those apartments and there's rooms there, a picture of daisies on the wall, maybe an old player piano. You see that there's life there, and it's nice — suddenly the place doesn't seem like an ant colony any more.

"But once you get that — really get things from all the angles — ant colonies one day and daisies the next day — it's too hard to believe in that one thing I was telling you about. Because you *know* now that life's full of shades and angles you hadn't thought about before — the used car salesman and the used car customer, if you know what I'm saying. Then it's too hard to feel sure and good about the one path you've picked for yourself, and if the world thinks you're a sorry sight, you'll agree with 'em. Do you see what I'm saying?"

I nodded as Louis sat back and relit his big cigar. Then he took a great haul out of it. He held the cigar straight up in the air from his mouth like the snorkeler I'd seen back at the Resorts. I would have given anything to have taken a picture of Louis right then. I felt like I could have asked him to sit a long while like that for a portrait.

The room around me looked like a place that had been settled by a childless, middle-class couple with bad taste who'd one day simply been beamed to another planet to make room for this group. The wood paneling on the walls was dotted with things hung too high up on them — a clock with a star bursting out of it, a calendar of Miss America beauties in their bikinis, which was as close to smut as the childless middle-class couple would have allowed in their home, a paint-by-number of a Siberian Tiger, framed in unfinished wood, and a needlepoint of "The Last Supper." I mentally thumbed through the figures in the house to decide who the place might have belonged to but came up empty-handed. Maybe it was some kind of hang-out one of them owned — maybe payment for a bad debt — and they all met here now and then to socialize.

"I was just wondering if I could use your bathroom," I said.

"Just down the hall," the former Rockette said, "on the right."

I had to excuse myself to get past the young girl, tossing hair bands, and she said, "Do you want to play?"

"No, I just need to use the facilities." She lowered her brown eyes, disappointed. "But maybe in a minute when I get done in there," I said.

"OK," she piped up.

The bathroom was small but quite clean. I quickly thumbed through the figures again to determine which one of them might have gone to the trouble. That was the strange thing. I couldn't stop myself wondering one thing or another in a house where no one worried too much about my life or my ambitions — have a swig here, a smoke there, talk for a while on the phone, wait for Ezio, drop a couple of pearls — and just get on with things without suspecting all the time that a war criminal might just have walked through your door. And the strange part was that I was sure these people had been around and seen a few things to make them suspicious, even the girl.

I did my business, then gawked in the mirror. I looked surprisingly fresh for a wet dog in the middle of the night and felt so comfortable that I did something I'd never done before: I picked up the hairbrush on the washstand, plucked a hair or two out of it, then ran it through my own hair.

When I got out, the girl was repeating, ". . . steamboat, steamboat, steamboat, steamboat —"

"What are you doing?" I asked.

"Well, you said you'd be a minute, and I hate putting steamboats in between my seconds when I count, so I put a whole bunch in the beginning; then I can count as fast as I want."

"Oh, that sounds like a good idea."

She handed me the four different-colored hair bands and said, "OK, you go first."

I aimed, then stopped and sauntered over to the peg, which was actually the end of a broom handle jammed into a cardboard panel. I studied it, picked a piece of lint off it — in short, made an ass of myself — probably because of the pressure I'd felt over the years from Clyde in these situations. I aimed again with the zebra-striped hair band, the only one which wasn't a solid color, and hurled it high up on the wall near the ceiling at the back of the corridor. It clattered almost all the way back to our feet.

"I guess I'm a little out of practise."

"That's OK. Try again," the girl said, and I decided I liked her right away.

I threw the other three, one after the other, and was glad there was a corridor to contain them. Then the girl picked them up, and I watched her, her thin arms and legs swimming around in her nightie.

All four of her shots came close, two of them ringing the peg dead on and settling down for a point. She gathered them up and handed them to me again. My turn. I wanted to ask her if she lived here but was afraid to cause a stir. "Do you know about music?" she asked me.

"*Music?* No, not much — just Every Good Boy Deserves Fudge, and I also know FACE."

She cackled her little head off when I said this. Then she settled down and asked if I wanted to see her room.

"Oh, you have a room here? — Sure." I realized right away how stupid that statement was, but she didn't seem bothered.

She asked me my name and told me hers was Kathleen as I followed her into what was, again, a small but tidy room filled with just what I would have expected: stuffed animals, board games on a shelf, a poster showing kittens in a basket, and a matched white vanity, dresser and bed.

"Listen to this," she said, and she pulled a recorder out of a case beneath her bed. She played "Early One Morning," then "When the Saints Go Marching In." And she did a dandy job with both tunes.

"You're very talented, Kathleen," I said and wondered if she'd taken music in school but again was afraid to ask. It was a first for me, but I was not sure I wanted to find out, really, how or when these nocturnal creatures got the regular life that kids got, nor did I think right away that I would have to save this thin-limbed girl from a fate which, on balance, did not look so bad — what with a pretty mother whose only crime might have been that she spent a little too long on the phone, and big Louis to look after her, and the former Rockette showing her a step or two, and all that gold for cash the retired pawnbroker must have stashed away for his friends here. It was an arrangement a few families I was acquainted with might have envied — that's for sure. And anyway who was I to be rescuing thin-legged people from anything? What could I pass on to them — some camera store lore or a pointer or two about Henry Fleming and what it meant for him to be going off to the Civil War with his jars of blackberry jam? It might even have been the arrangement Bunny knew best in her childhood. I suddenly warmed tremendously to the little girl here.

"Where did you learn to play like that?" I asked.

"From my mum. She's a singer, and she's very good. She bought me this book and showed me how to play."

She killed me with her little Noo Joisey accent. "That's terrific," I said.

"Look," she said. She was pointing to a small, framed,

black-and-white photo on the far wall, then got up to get it for me. It was a picture of Kathleen's mother, Ray Charles and *Bunny*!

"Oh, my God!" I said.

"Yeah, I know," Kathleen said. "It's Ray Charles. My mum knows lots of famous people."

"No — I mean, yeah, that's great. But that's Bunny Tremaine with them."

"Yeah, she's an old friend of my mum's."

"Oh, really? Do you know much about her? Do you know where she lives?"

Kathleen shrugged her shoulders. Then her face brightened. "I could find out for you." She was hugging the small picture against her chest. "If my mum ever gets off the phone, or if you come visit me tomorrow, I could find out for you. Will you do that, Eddie?"

"I don't know." Kathleen looked disappointed. "I mean, I'm not from around here, so I don't even know if I'd find my way back to this place, and even if I did, I'm not sure I'd be welcome again — you know how it is."

"Oh, everyone's welcome here. I'm sure everyone out in the living room likes you a lot already."

I could easily have hugged her right then, she was smiling so broadly. I wanted to introduce her to the Taj Mahal doorman and swing them both around a bit. I wanted to tell her about the Canada Geese and about the hoods who stole my car, but I didn't want to unsettle her this late at night, so I just smiled back with the same warmth.

Kathleen walked across the room to rehang the photo, then sighed as she sat back down on her bed beside me. She bounced a bit to rev up her engines again. "*I* know! Why don't you come visit me at my school! That would be the best! My school has a soldier at it with a bayonet."

"A *bayonet?*"

"Yep. And he's bigger and meaner than anyone else you've ever seen."

"Wow," I said. "And what grade are you in?"

"Sixth." Kathleen was starting to look sleepy now and yawned widely to emphasize the point. I could see all her little, white teeth and the two, bigger adult ones in the front.

"Do you know anyone famous?" she asked.

"Well, let me see. No one as famous as Ray Charles — boy, that's really something. I think the only really famous person I've ever known was the Father of the Cheesie."

"The *Cheesie?*"

"Yeah — you know — Cheesies — Cheese Doodles — whatever. His son was a friend of mine in school. One day, even before my friend was born, his father-to-be cooked up a kettle of them and sold the patent soon after. He hasn't worked another day since. It hasn't helped him that much — except for getting rich, I mean. He kind of sits around in a nice big house — my friend's father, I mean — and drinks a lot of beer. That's about it. But he's left his little mark, and I guess that's something, too."

"Wow," she said. Her eyes glistened with the thought. "I love Cheese Doodles."

"Yeah, me, too. And you could do much worse than invent Cheesies. For instance, you could be the person who came up with the short form for the word 'at.' Do you know that one — the *a* with the circle around it? I mean, it seems to me 'at' is already pretty short and probably didn't need the help." Kathleen gave me a puzzled look. "Anyway, let me see, who else? I also know Bunny Tremaine, your mom's friend. She might be famous someday soon."

"My mum knows famous people. She knows everyone that sings. She's met loads of singers — *live*. I only know a couple of them because I sometimes meet them backstage or whatever."

"Well, maybe I should ask her then, when she gets off the phone — about Bunny, I mean."

"She must know her. She knows *everyone* — Wayne Newton, Al Martino, Buddy Greco. She even sang a duet once with Wayne Newton. It was a song called 'The Lady is a Tramp.'"

"Boy, Wayne Newton. That must have been special for her."

Kathleen looked into my eyes and I looked into hers, then we cracked up. It was one of those rare moments you have with people, the kind that pop up as your life passes before your eyes on your dying day.

She put her thin arms around my neck, kissed my cheek, then let go. "You should ask my mum about Bunny anyways, but I think I'm going to sleep now," she said and, being dressed for it, slipped right into bed.

"Good night," I said, but she'd dropped off immediately after she'd gotten comfortable, so I switched off the light and left.

I was reeling when I walked out again into the living room. The only thing missing from this happy circumstance was Ezio. He arrived about a minute after I'd sat down in my original chair — just as my need to call

173

Brenda to explain what had happened to me faded and was replaced by an outrageously strong desire to see Kathleen again, to call her someday maybe or send her something — a nice tape of the world's best recorder players — something. And it was then, just as I was unexpectedly overcome with emotion, that Ezio walked in.

He really was the last word in pants, this Ezio. He'd brought along a dozen pairs of the world's finest — in silk, leather, cool wool — you name it. He also had a bag of Chinese food, a carton of cigarettes and a bag of cocaine. Ezio was like an Atlantic City Santa Claus and might even have swooped in from the South Pole the way he dropped things left and right: the smokes for the Rockette, the pants for Louis, the food and drugs for anyone who felt like reaching for them.

The Louis Armstrong stand-in dropped his big pants, and I noticed right away that the ones Ezio had brought were all in his size. With Ezio's help, he pulled on a pair of the gray silk ones.

The woman on the phone said into it, "Ezio's here. I gotta go in a minute." It was the first thing I'd heard her say, she'd been speaking so quietly up until that point, and I finally wondered who it was she could have been speaking to — for a mad moment, I thought she might even have been talking to Bunny — but whoever it was, he or she knew Ezio as well as anyone.

"So what d'ya think?" Louis said to everyone, turning like a fashion model. Ezio was on his knees, fussing with the cuffs. The retired pawnbroker took an immense snort of white powder into one of his nostrils, using a hollow pen he'd brought along for the occasion. He offered me the pen and the bag, but I declined politely. Running the strange hairbrush through my hair was as far as I was willing to go on this night.

"You look like a prince," said the former Rockette, pointing an egg roll at Louis while crushing out her cigarette with her other hand. "Hey, Ezio," she said, an alfalfa sprout hanging out of the side of her mouth, wriggling like an insect, "do you have any of those leggings in that trunk of yours? You promised me some green or pink leggings — did you forget?"

"Honey," Ezio said with a couple of pins in his mouth, "have I evah fahgotten you? — Tell me dat."

"Once you did. Once you forgot that top you promised me."

"I didn't fahget da top. How many times I gotta tell ya? Fah da last time, my suppliah was outta dose tops — I told ya dat. Did I not get one in special for yous not two days latah from Noo Yowak? Fahget about it ahready. Jus' hold on dere and munch on that egg roll o' yoahs, or have a zip or two of yoah drink, I'll be right back wit' da leggings, all right?" And Ezio crawled over and kissed her all the way up her leg to where her short skirt ended. She purred like an old cat.

Just then, Kathleen's mother got off the phone, walked into the room with us, and looked through the bag of Chinese food. She said, "Did you bring any of those — watchamacallems? — those chow maim noodles?"

"I brought everyting. Jus' keep lookin'." She gazed up at me for an instant with a look exactly like her daughter's when I'd told Kathleen how talented she was. My mouth was wide open, ready to ask her about Bunny, when she

175

walked back into the kitchen with her noodles, picked up the phone right away and made another call.

I realized then that I'd just blown it. If I was going to make any calls to Clyde or Bunny *or the police* — come to think of it, not the police — I'd missed the boat. It would be morning before the phone was free again, so — just like that — I leaned over to the retired pawnbroker and told him I thought I ought to be going. I asked if he knew the way back to the casinos.

"What's your hurry?" he said. "Have an egg roll."

"No, I should go. I had my car stolen right out from under me tonight, so I think I should go report it or something."

"Hey." He looked up at Louis, who had on a pair of brown serge pants now. "Didja hear that?"

"What?" Ezio glanced over, too. He was kneeling on the floor and looked as tiny as a child.

"This kid had his car swiped tonight."

Everyone laughed again.

"What kind of car was it, kid?" Louis asked.

"A Cadillac Allanté."

"Ooo-la-la," said Ezio. "Fahget about it ahready."

"Get it back for him," the former Rockette said.

"Get it *back* for me?" I asked.

"Sure, why not?" Louis said. "Let me just finish off with these pants, and we'll scout around a bit. It's a small town, no big deal."

The pawnbroker put his worry beads in his pocket and pulled out some keys. "What did the guys look like?" he asked me.

"One of them had his face crossed out."

The pawnbroker reached into his pocket, pulled out a switchblade, snapped out the blade and asked, "Like this?" He drew a faint line down across his own face.

"Yeah, *exactly*. How did you know?"

"That Ortiz'll nevah loin," Ezio said, his mouth full of pins.

"Ortiz has a slash like that?" I asked.

"No, Ortiz has a ball growin' out of the side of his head. Did you see a guy with a ball out of the side of his head?"

I nodded, and within five minutes we were in the back of the black Lincoln, with white Louis beside me and the retired pawnbroker and Ezio in front. I told them my whole story, beginning with Bunny and Almond but leaving out the bits about my crying, and the pawnbroker zeroed in on Almond. "Was he a short, kinda tough guy — black hair?"

"That's exactly what he was."

Ezio asked, "Was he fast wit his fingahs — do a lot of hocus-pocus, possibly?"

"That's Almond," I said, amazed at what a small world I'd stumbled into.

"No, dat's not Almond," Ezio said. "It's *Almonetti*, but let's fahget about him jus' fah now. We'll give him some tought latah. Let's get dat vehicle back fah you foist."

We screeched left past The Way of Life Assembly of God Church and tore down Ventnor Avenue in the direction I thought the taxi had gone. "Try the Eye of the Needle," Louis said. He had his handkerchief on the seat between us.

We rode along like maniacs, practically forcing one car off the road as we turned up a dark main street. I tried to orient myself, as if that were possible, and looked out the window at the street signs whipping by — Martin Luther King Jr. Avenue, I caught, then Baltic and Mediterranean, then, finally Magellan and Absecon, where we seemed to be settling down to stop. And that was it — The Eye of the Needle Saloon. And sitting there in the lot, staring smartly and redly at me, was Clyde's Allanté!

"They always hang out heah," said Ezio.

We sauntered in, which was really the only way to walk into a place like The Eye of the Needle, and there they were right in front of us: Ortiz and the crossed-out guy, having a beer with the customary plate of fries and gravy shoved off to the side. I didn't see the other two anywhere. It was only now as Louis crossed in front of me that I noticed he was still wearing the pair of brown serge pants, pinned up at the bottom.

We walked right up to Ortiz's table and hovered over the two men, though Louis, on account of his size, was better at hovering than the rest of us. Then Ezio did the most disgusting thing: he picked out one of the fries soaked in gravy from Ortiz's plate and slurped it into his mouth. I knew he was doing it largely for effect, but it was disgusting all the same.

The retired pawnbroker did all the talking. "I understand you boys have some new keys. What'sa matter? Joe's garage not open yet for business?" He took out his switchblade and snapped it open all in the same motion. I looked over my shoulder at the bartender who didn't seem too bothered by what was happening. Ortiz and the crossed-out guy didn't look up. They were trying to pretend we weren't there. The retired pawnbroker scratched the side of his nose with the blade. "You've offended my friend, Little Pippy of Canada here. He's a visitor, and he has not been treated so nicely this evening by our tourist bureau, now has he?"

I wasn't sure I appreciated the Little Pippy crack, particularly since I could do a bit of hovering myself over both the former pawnbroker and Ezio, but I didn't want to seem ungrateful, so I let the comment pass.

Ortiz made a motion with the lump on his head, and the crossed-out guy pulled out the familiar key-chain with the red rabbit's foot attached to it. "We were just having some fun with our little friend," Ortiz said.

I puffed out my chest just to show how big I was, and then the retired pawnbroker said, "Any other effects we need to worry about?"

"I don't think so, main."

"No wallets, no jewelry, no —"

"OK, OK. Give him the watch and wallet, main."

Main took my watch out of his side pocket and my wallet out of his pants pocket, but it looked thicker than I'd ever seen it. He started to pull some notes out of it, but out of nowhere Ezio was there, snatching the bundle out of main's hand. He handed it all to me behind him, without even glancing back, and then I heard Louis take a whole westerly of air into his lungs before saying, "Let's go," as if he were fending off some switchblade action that I guess he could see coming.

We filed out the door, not one of us taking a backward glance. Outside, I looked into the wallet and quickly noticed at least six one-hundred-dollar notes inside. "I don't know how to thank you gentlemen," I sputtered.

"But would you at least take this money? It's not even mine."

"Keep it," Louis said with a big grin. I was expecting him any second to break into the refrain from *Hello, Dolly*. "It's for the aggravation."

"No, please, I insist." I was holding out the hundreds, but Louis and the retired pawnbroker were already headed for their black Lincoln. "Please," I said again.

Ezio snatched one of the hundreds — he was really very good with that snatching motion of his — and said, "ok, maybe fa da Chinese food, but fahget about it ahready." He gave my face a few soft slaps. Then he scooted off to the Lincoln after the others. His parting words were: "We won't fahget Almonetti eider. Don't give it anoddah tought."

"Thank you very much," I said, "but you've been kind enough already. You saved my hide there. You don't really have to go after Almond . . . etti."

"No trouble at all," he said as he climbed into the car.

"What I mean is —"

"Don't mention it."

The former pawnbroker had already fired up the engine. He rolled down his window. "Follow us," he said. "We'll get you outta here."

"Oh, I can't tell you how much I appreciate that. I have to get back down to Merv's hotel."

I jumped into Clyde's car, which stank of Brut, and followed the Lincoln out into the street. The retired pawnbroker was nicer about keeping an eye on me than Brenda had been and drove slowly until we got out to what looked like Atlantic Avenue again. Then he slowed almost to a stop, honked, and I followed his arm out the window as he gestured upwards at the red-lighted letters of the Resorts. When I looked down again, the Lincoln was gone. In the distance, I heard a screech and gave my horn a good smart farewell blast.

Chapter Thirteen

A cheerful doorwoman was there for me like an angel, though I would even have settled for the usual glum guy, and the cardboard cutout of Merv by the door felt now like a friendly, old uncle. I whooshed up to my room, swung open the door, ready to hug anyone there, felt slightly deflated to find no one and both beds all rumpled, turned on the stadium lights and saw my old pal, *The Red Badge of Courage*, on the night table where Bunny might have left it, open on its belly, waiting for my return. Our digital clock read 5:55, and I let out a great sigh as I realized I no longer had to call the police or Brenda, who was no doubt fast asleep by now, or Clyde, though I would eventually have to explain the disappearance of *Oklahoma* and *Guys and Dolls*.

The one other thing on my mind was the hundreds of dollars of stolen money in my wallet and the poor sap Ortiz and the boys must have held up to get it, a guy who might very well have been wandering around the way I had been. I felt a strange kind of kinship with the fellow — or it might even have been a girl — what *else* might they have done to a poor girl, especially if she was a crier like me? I thought maybe I should take out an ad in *The Press*, telling whoever it was that I had his money, so he should meet me at the hotel — maybe in the lobby would be best. But then who would answer such an ad? Half the citizens of Atlantic City and maybe a few from Philadelphia. Maybe even Ortiz and his crossed-out friend would be in the line-up which would stretch out the door and several blocks up North Carolina Avenue. No — no ad.

I could give the money to Ted, lying there with his ashtray, back at The Way of Life Assembly of God Church — if I could ever find the place again. Maybe I could help him get back to his girlfriend in Wisconsin. Or maybe he'd try out his hand at the tables again. Besides, I was sure his brother in Toledo would have bailed him out by now. What kind of brother would let him just lie there on a church floor in Atlantic City?

In any case, whichever of the four of us — the other robbery victim, Ted, the damaged head gang or I — ended up with the money, it belonged rightfully to no one; there was no justice to be corrected because this was Atlantic City where cars banged together and drove away, where roulette made more sense than justice.

I strolled around our room. Oh, how good it felt to be back! I wanted now to hop into that whirlpool and French-mill my body until it sang. I wanted the world to know what I had been through, what streets I'd wandered, what people I'd met away from the safety of these walls which were once hospital walls gazed upon for solace and mercy by the wounded of the war.

I tore off my damp clothes, dropped them at my feet, switched on the sun-lamp, leaned over to turn on one of the four taps, lost my footing on a wet towel which had lain curled on the floor, plummeted head-first into the deep and friendly tub and blacked out.

When I came to, I was doubled over the side of the tub with my bare buns tanning in the sun-lamp. I peeked around the corner and was grateful to discover I was still alone. It was after 7:00. My head throbbed. I looked in the mirror to find a lump on my forehead which rivaled Ortiz's. I asked myself my name to see if I was still all there, then staggered over to my bed, climbed in and drifted into a bright and cheerful sleep.

When I woke up, a wet face cloth was draped over my forehead. Clyde was asleep in the bed beside me. The clock said 4:15, but I honestly couldn't tell what day it was, or whether it was morning or night because the million-dollar curtains of our room were closed. I stared for a minute at Clyde and wanted to hate his snoring, black Elvis head, but I found I couldn't on account of the face cloth on my forehead. That's just the way I was. I swear, if I'd been out in the trenches on a battlefield, gawked through my binoculars and saw an enemy soldier pouring his pal a cup of tea out of a thermos, then patting him on the shoulder, I would have climbed out of my trench to surrender. I am the world's biggest sucker for small gestures. My head no longer hurt, but I was still tired, so I rolled over and went back to sleep.

When I got up again, Clyde was gone. It was 7:30, the maid had not been in, probably because Clyde hadn't bothered about hanging the "Chambermaid, please make up the room now!" tag on the door, so I thought I would now gingerly head into the bathroom and try that bath again.

It was then, just as I was whirling around in the tub, happy as a goose in a pond, that I got that feeling again like that heart attack of my grandfather's which hovered over my head, except it wasn't pain I felt this time but grief. A fear came over me right there in that swirling tub that I had lost something, but because I have no way of dialing directly into these feelings, I could not know whether it was Clyde I had lost, the happy little doorman at the Taj Mahal, the young girl I'd tossed hair bands with, or Ricky, the hamster. All I knew was that there was a general sagging in my chest, like the feeling that comes with grief.

It was the same sensation as the one I'd had another time when I was ten and watched my grandmother, my father's mother, being lowered into the ground while people hurled flowers into the hole after her. I dreamt about her for years afterward, and each time I did, I felt that hollowness in my chest. Once, when I was older and Clyde was already in business, my grandmother visited me in my sleep. She told me that Clyde was making Jane and himself unhappy. He should speak earnestly with her. The following day, I told Clyde about the sunken feeling I sometimes got and that our grandmother had taken the trouble to come visit me. Then I told him what she'd said.

"I didn't pay any attention to her when she was alive," he answered. "Why should I listen to her now that she's dead?"

So, even if I were to round up Clyde now and tell him how I felt, he'd tell me to get that lump on my head looked at. But I had no choice. The feeling would not go away.

I jumped out of the tub and dried myself off but, just as I was doing so, I glanced in the mirror and noticed a white hair, lounging right along with the red ones in a wave flowing down across the lump on my forehead. How could it have grown in so fast? Or if it hadn't, why hadn't I noticed it before? I thought for a second that it might have been left there by the brush I'd used back at big Louis' place, but when I tried to tug it out, it held its ground. I got dressed in some new clothes I yanked out of my bag and put on one of Clyde's sports jackets because my reversible jacket needed some mending — what a job, come to think of it, Ezio would have done with it if I'd handed it over for a minute or two. I was on my way in a flash.

Clyde was not in the casino nor the oyster bar beside it, nor the Hollywood Grill above it. I ran out to the Boardwalk and over to the Taj Mahal, not knowing now if it was twilight I was seeing or the half light of dawn. The doorman was not there, intensifying my fear. I ran like a madman up and down the aisles of the casino, knocking out the long feather in the headdress of one of the harem waitresses, but I did not see him. I bolted up and down the carpeted halls of the building, pausing at the Alhambra. The show card was missing! I tried to pull open the door, but it was locked. A man dressed in blue overalls came up from behind and asked if I'd brought the right nuts.

"The *what*?"

"The nuts for the pipes." I kept looking at him, wondering now if I was still asleep back in my room. "For the leaky pipes in the ceiling," he said.

"Oh, the *nuts*," I said, backing down the hall.

It was not until I was heading out the back door toward the Boardwalk that I glimpsed Clyde through the window of the New Delhi Deli. I don't ever remember feeling so relieved. I bound up the steps, broke past the maitre d' and caught my breath before making my way over to his table.

He was sitting with his arm around Pretti!

"Where have you *been?*" I asked.

"What the hell are you talking about?" He lowered his arm. "What do you think you're doing wearing my jacket and what the hell happened to your stupid head? I thought for a while there that you'd left me and gone back home."

Pretti said, "Bobby, do you *know* Teddy here?"

"*Eddie,*" I said, "and yes he does." I thought of telling Pretti about the former Rockette I'd run into, but I was not in the right frame of mind. "Now, where is Bunny — can you tell me that?"

Pretti said, "Maybe I should go."

"Maybe you should," I said, sliding in on the other side of Clyde. "My brother and I have some things to talk over."

"Stay where you are," Clyde said.

"Don't talk to me like that — *either* of you," Pretti said, and she moved an inch or two away from Clyde.

I took a spoon in my hands and began twirling it around. We sat in silence for a moment. I got up to leave again when I heard a soft, familiar voice behind me. "Eddie, are you all right?" It was Bunny.

I turned and said the first thing that popped into my mind. "Do you happen to know where the doorman who works here got to? Do you know where he could be?"

Clyde said, "I think this boy needs a doctor. Are there any in the hotel here?" He was talking to both women.

"I'm just fine, thank you. All I asked was where the goddamn doorman was. Is that so sick?"

"No, it isn't," Bunny said. "He's taken a day off, that's all. He is a very nice man, isn't he?" She laid a hand on my shoulder, and I peered over in time to see the whites of Clyde's eyes.

"Eddie, what on earth happened to your head?" Bunny ran the cool tips of her fingers over the surface of the lump. She had a green and earthy smell.

"Oh, it's a long story," I said.

Pretti suddenly piped up: "Isn't this place just fabulin? It's got practically every show in the world right at your doorstep."

Clyde had his camel look on again, but I think all of us were looking at her in a goofy way. "Yes, it sure is," I finally said. "My favorite show, though, is the Jane and Jeffy Show. You really should try to catch it sometime. It's truly terrifin. It's a ventriloquist act."

"Hey," Pretti said. "Are you being sarcastic?"

"Yeah," Clyde said. "Why don't you just shut your mouth — and where the hell do you get off wearing my jacket, I asked you!"

"Boy, you really —" I tossed the spoon back onto the table and spoke over its clattering — "you really get around, don't you, Bob?"

"I don't think that's any of your goddamn business, now, is it?"

I felt I was going to cry again, or possibly even faint. I pulled off the jacket, bunched it up, threw it in Clyde's face and took off, turning once to see Bunny's shocked face.

Even before I got back to the room, I realized my keys and wallet were still in Clyde's herringbone, so I slumped against the wall outside our room and tried to review what had just happened, but all I could remember was the sensation of Bunny's cool fingers on my forehead, the image of her, sylph-like in white underclothing, the skin electrified, the jolt of her nipples through her brassiere, charged by the phantom Frank in her high school hall — by *Clyde* who was hardly trying — the buttery voice spooning out "Georgia on my Mind," the eyes green and tropical. What was it about those sweet, green Hispanic eyes, that green fragrance, the velvety voice that got to me — bore into me — followed me wherever I went along the watery streets of this Atlantis of Wonder and Merriment? What hovel had she looked out of all those years, gazing at night walkers who had wandered off the beaten track? Or when the Miss Fifty States zoomed by, smiling for the cameras as they hung off the side of that red bus? Something about her reassured me in the way the ocean had as it tossed back the plastic cups and world famous salt water taffy wrappers, warmed my heart the way that young Kathleen, throwing hair bands and playing "Early One Morning" on her recorder, had warmed me, bound me in the same kind of spell in which I'd seen Bunny bound by Almond. How many holy wafers could be thrown my way before I snatched one out of the air and chomped right down on it? And who had it been that had met her, bedded her down, won her heart?

And then I fainted. I had a vision or a dream — whatever one has when one has not voluntarily gone to sleep — of Desmond Pencil, my lucky charm, dressed as the Pied Piper, sporting a three-corned hat with a feather, leading Jeffy and Kathleen and even the boy with the French fries and gravy back at Barclay's Saloon down the Boardwalk, all of them dancing as Desmond played "Old Man River" on his flute and the kids sang along. They walked toward a distant, red, magic bus parked on the shore, and as they neared their destination, suddenly Jeffy was wearing a black tuxedo with tails and his hair was greased like Bert Parks's hair. No, more like Bob Barker's, the young Bob Barker I'd seen in reruns, hosting *Truth or Consequences* — and Kathleen was in an evening gown with a sash that read — I couldn't quite make it out until she twirled to the song and I could see her tears of joy and flashbulbs going off — it read, "Miss New Jersey."

They boarded the bus. I tried to call out but my voice caught in my throat. I flailed madly. By the time I managed a squawk, the bus had turned toward the busy ocean and disappeared beneath the waves.

Chapter Fourteen

When I awoke, I thought I was in our hotel room, but it was a hospital room. I had a bandage wrapped around my forehead. For a moment, I felt relieved because I'd bought into that hopeless and unreal dream and was glad to find that it wasn't true. Then I heard the sound of voices and the clinking of glasses. I lifted my head off the pillow.

"How you feeling now?" Bunny said. She was sitting in a chair beside the bed. Clyde was at the end of my bed with Pretti beside him in another chair. She was drawing small circles with a finger on his knee.

"I'm feeling fine."

"What happened to you anyway?" asked Bunny.

"It's a long story," I said. "Let's just say that, since I last saw you, I've been skulking and lurking and flailing around the streets of this city, becoming acquainted with some of its fine citizens."

Clyde said, "Did you flail head-first into a tree or something?"

"Very amusing," I said. Pretti giggled.

"What, then?" Clyde asked. "Were you in a brawl?"

"Something like that," I said and felt the bandage on my forehead. "Actually, I coco-butted some wild beast in an alley who had attacked my honor."

Everyone waited for more, but quickly let it pass. Clyde slid an inch or two away from Pretti and looked at Bunny. "We weren't sure there for a while," he said. "It was touch and go. I thought maybe you'd slipped into a coma or some damn thing. These two ladies graciously agreed to keep me company in my hour of need." I was ready to puke. "By the way," he said, "where'd you get all this money?" He pointed to my wallet on the bedside table. The herringbone jacket was draped over the back of Bunny's chair.

I sat right up before realizing I had on one of those backless hospital gowns. "What the hell were you doing — going through my things?"

"No, he wasn't," Pretti said. "Now, to be fair —" she held up her finger — "it fell out when Bobby put the jacket down, that's all."

"Anyway, I was right proud of you," Clyde said, and it was *exactly* the way he said it — *right proud* — like some kind of plantation owner. "I thought maybe you'd picked up a couple of tricks from the Blackjack Warrior."

"No, blackjack's not my game," I said.

"I have a great idea for a game!" Pretti said, springing to her feet, clapping her hands together and shaking out her stunned auburn hair.

"I don't think I want to play anything," Bunny said, taking a breathy swig of her drink. "I think I just want to know what happened to Eddie's head. I'm kind of tired, to tell you the truth."

Clyde got up to freshen everyone's drink. He poured me one too out of a 40-ouncer he'd brought with him. "Hey, I wonder if we can ask for some ice around here," he said, using a cool little wrist action like a bartender to pretend he was plunking a couple of cubes into the glasses.

"Come on, why don't we have a go at this game?" Pretti said again. "I'm not talking about canasta, for goodness' sake; I'm talking about this fabulin game I played once at a party out in L.A."

I sat up in bed, genuinely curious. Bunny helped arrange the pillows behind me, and I felt her nail lightly scratch my bare back. I could smell her floral, mossy perfume. I couldn't have been happier that she was there right then.

"It's called *Cringers*," Pretti said, "and it's really superb, trust me." I took my drink from Clyde who smiled at me confidentially, almost, the way he does when we're alone.

"The rules are very simple, really," Pretti went on. She was still on her feet, and she began moving around and talking like a gym teacher. "You need to tell us a true story about yourself, a story that makes your skin crawl just to remember it. It should *not* be a story about your nylons running, or having a piece of spinach caught in your teeth the night of a first date, but a *real cringer* — what do you guys think?"

A woman's voice came over the hospital P.A., calling for a Dr. Petrie who was needed in cardiology. We all paused to listen, even Pretti who stopped pacing. I could hear the fall wind off the ocean, touching off an eerie howling and I sat up erect to peek outside. I realized I was starving and would have given anything for an Almond Joy or Oh Henry. Clyde stretched out his long, competitive legs across the bed beside me.

"I don't know if I want to bother with this," Bunny said. "I don't see the point, really, Prett'."

"Well, there is no *point*," Pretti said. She was still pacing in the small circle created by my bed and the two chairs. The window creaked and howled. Pretti had a spidery quality to her walk. "What point is there to any game? It'll be fun, that's all. It'll cheer us all up." She shot out her arms now, like a cheerleader. "We all have *something* to really cringe about, you'll see. D'you know what — I'll start, and you'll get what I mean."

Pretti raised her hands to her lips as if in prayer and said, "This happened two years ago — do you remember, Bun', when I went out to L.A. to see what dancing jobs I could find? I met that guy named Tony and got engaged to him right away?" Bunny was nodding. "Anyway, I was too young, but there you have it." Clyde took a big swig from his brandy glass. "We were living together, this guy — my fiancé — and I, and Tony was not a bad guy, really — he was everything I could have asked for in bed, that's for sure. The guy could keep it up for hours. Anyway — anyway — he was fabulinly dull." Pretti squeezed in again beside Clyde on the bed. "Really, there are some people who should never leave bed. They're created just for you-know-what, I swear. This guy spent whatever time he wasn't working, watching the Raiders or reading the sports pages or spouting Dodgers statistics or, for God's sake, throwing around a ball with his pals at the park." I could see Clyde's face flushing, from his neck upwards and I wondered whether it was the brandy. "There was no end to it," Pretti said, "sports and beer, that was his life. And *bed*, of course. It was too bad he proposed to me in bed, catching me at a weak moment. I did love him a little, I guess, really, but not enough to spend the rest of my life with the guy. Anyway, what happened," she said, interrupting herself to finish off her own brandy — she was up on her knees again, and the bed was rocking — "was that I started seeing someone else. I had feelings for Tony, honestly, really, but he did not understand the life of a dancer — not that I had much of one at the time — I mostly waited on tables — but you know what I mean." Pretti was looking at *me*, of all people. She now settled on the bed again, languidly stretching out her dancer's legs alongside Clyde's. She had on a black leotard and an open white blouse. I looked over at Bunny, who was wearing the white dress I'd met her in, and took a breath.

"Anyway," Pretti went on, "I never wanted to hurt Tony, but I started messing around with Nick, my boss at that Pelican Restaurant I told you about, Bun'?"

"Yes, I remember," Bunny said. Her eyes followed Pretti's mouth, then traced a line along Clyde's outstretched legs until she glanced over at me and quickly down at her drink.

"Anyway, it was just one of those things that happened, really. I started fooling around with Nick, and it was my birthday. Tony was out of town selling computers up in Seattle or some damn place, and he wasn't supposed to be back for several days. I didn't even *know* he knew it was my birthday — I don't ever remember mentioning it — so Nick and I had the run of the place. We could just as easily have gone over to his place, really, it was that simple, but mine was closer, that was all. So here's what happens: Nick drives me home from my shift that night. He can hardly control himself — the hairy animal — we step in the door and I don't even have a chance to get the lights on, he's already mauling me all over, pulling my shirt out of my pants, tweaking my nipples. Then — *bang* — the lights go on, and all Tony's and my friends are yelling, 'Surprise! Happy Birthday!' And there I stand in all my glory — my lipstick smeared, the back of my T-shirt tucked into my bra. And there stands Tony, *really*, holding one of those party-favor things you blow into that uncoils like a cobra. Nick takes off like a jack rabbit and leaves me standing there with Tony and all our friends. Oh, God. . . ." Pretti cupped her face in her hands.

Clyde sat up straight, lifted his brandy glass and ran his finger along the rim. I looked first at Clyde's face, then Bunny's, to see if anyone was feeling sorry for Pretti. I took a long swig out of my own glass and felt the liquor burn a path down my chest.

Pretti polished off her drink, held out her glass for more and began drinking again just as soon as Clyde had finished pouring. "Why don't *you* go now?" she said to Clyde, her voice a little throaty. "We'll alternate: girl-boy-girl-boy."

"I don't think I'm ready just yet."

"Come on — it's fun," she said, as if urging him into a cold swimming pool.

"No, I don't think so," Clyde said. "Why doesn't someone else go?" His face was shiny and red. "I'll think of something, but have someone else go in the meantime." He was looking directly at me.

"OK, I'll go again," Pretti said.

"Boy," Bunny said, leaning forward in her chair, and watching her drink swirl around at the bottom of her hospital glass. "You'll keep cringing here, Prett', until there's nothing left of you. I'll go," she said. I was taken aback.

"Good," Pretti said, and she bopped right back down into the other chair. Clyde let out a deep breath.

Before Bunny could start, a friendly nurse stuck her head into the room. "How we doin' here?" she asked.

"Much better," Pretti said. "See? He's sitting right up now."

"Yes, thank you," I said. "I'm much better."

"That's quite a nasty bump you took," the nurse said, coming right into the room and scattering Clyde and Pretti to their feet as she fixed the blankets. Clyde hid the bottle behind his back as Pretti cupped her hands around her glass. She looked as if she'd caught a firefly.

The nurse shot them a look before saying, "I'm going off shift now, Mr. Markson, but another nurse will be by later to give you something to help you sleep," she said and winked before turning to leave.

Everyone waited until she was well on her way before settling down again. Then Bunny got to her feet with her brandy. "I don't know if this qualifies as a cringer," she said, "but I'll give it a try, and you can tell me." I could see her heart beating through the light material of her dress. Her hands began to tremble around the glass.

Clyde stood to load up her glass again, and then she started. "I wanted to become a singer for a very long time. Nothing else mattered to me when I was young. We weren't well off — I mean, we weren't eating up the household pets for dinner or anything, but we weren't too well off. And I used to spend all the money I could get from my mother — and it wasn't much, that I can tell you — on Diana Ross records. Once I got a recording of an old Billie Holiday album, which I cherished and handled like a newborn. I'd put it on really carefully, then sing along. Boy, could I sing my little guts out when no one was watching!"

197

Bunny took a little sip, and we all followed suit. "I got my big break while I was still attending Atlantic City High."

"Is that the place across from the War Memorial?" I asked.

"Yes," Bunny said. "How did you know?"

"Oh, I've been around."

She smiled before saying, "I saw an ad for tryouts with this New York agent, and my mother took me down to this old community hall not far from my neighborhood. Except this New York guy was not so much an agent as an act himself, and he was looking for other, cheap acts to warm up a crowd before he himself went on. Anyway, that's not really the point of my story. I was picked out of 36 people that afternoon to tour with the guy and see what I could get going — as far as a singing career was concerned, I mean. My mother was so against it because I was just 17, and we had quite a traditional home — Pretti will vouch for me on that one."

Pretti giggled. "I'll say," she said.

"Anyway, things have been going along fairly smoothly these past five years — as far as my singing is concerned, I mean — but my personal life has been for the birds."

Bunny looked directly into my eyes, sat in her chair again, then gazed down into her lap. I thought she was going to cry. "Then one night, I'm doing my show as usual, and later I decide to participate in my manager's act just for a lark," she went on, still keeping her head down. "I had done it lots of times before." Her voice hitched. She kept glancing up. She was talking entirely to me now.

"I'd seen Pretti do it the night before, and it seemed like it'd be fun to give it a try — that's all — what harm could come of it? Then suddenly, I'm up on stage, falling into a trance, but I mean *really*, and I could feel myself, for the very first time in my life, being drawn outward, but I don't mean by the spell — by a pair of magnetic eyes out there in the darkness watching me — and I don't know what to do to stop myself from being pulled that way, but before I can think very much more about it, I slip away, and, bang, I'm back in high school trying to get noticed, long before my singing days have begun."

A tear splashed down onto Bunny's stockinged knee as she hunched forward. She tried to brush it off. Clyde got up to go to the table by my side to hand Bunny a Kleenex. He looked puzzled but said nothing. Pretti had her heels up on her chair and her knees up to her chin and was bobbing a little against them.

"Then later on that night," Bunny continued, "I don't even know how much later, I must really have been out of it, though I remember the sensation of someone warming me — sheltering me, I guess I mean — and taking me away. The next thing I know — it's morning, and I'm back in the room I'd slept in the night before, except in the other bed, and there's no one else there with me though it *felt* like someone *was*, it's really wild. All I know is —" and Bunny looked directly at me again as she scrunched the damp Kleenex in her hand. Once again, her face colored over with that beautiful, stricken, tragic look I'd fallen in love with, the ringlets of hair framing that face as striking as if they'd been drawn by hand. "All I know is," she said, "that someone — or it certainly *felt* like someone — someone very nice finally took me away from my estranged husband."

I shot out of bed to my feet. I felt a brief spell of wooziness come over me. "Your husband!"

"My *estranged* husband. I'm sorry, Eddie. What would you have said if I'd told you this at our table before going on? What would you have thought? I don't think I could have survived the look on your face. I'm sorry if you feel deceived now, but better this than —"

"Than what?" I said.

"Can someone please tell me what the hell is going on here?" Clyde said. He looked at me.

"No," I said. "Why don't *you* tell us what is going on?" I was still on my feet. "Why don't you run one of your cringers past us first. I'm sure you'll be the evening's champion, as usual." I sat back down again, leaned back and crossed my arms.

"Eddie, why don't you just —"

"No," Pretti said. She took hold of Clyde's elbow. "None of that now. We're having a friendly game here. Go ahead now, Bobby. You do one now, and then we'll have Eddie, OK? But no fights — that's not what this is about."

I glanced at Bunny who was holding her tiny, wet Kleenex up against her nose, looking vacantly out at the floor. Then she got to her feet and said, "I'm going."

"Oh, come on," Pretti said. "We're just getting warmed up here. Stay a while longer."

Bunny thought a moment and reluctantly folded herself back into her chair with her drink. We all watched and said nothing.

"All right, I'll go now," Clyde said, trying to perk up the room the way Pretti had. He made his way to the middle of the floor as if doing so had become part of the rules.

"Let me see here," he said.

Clyde poured himself some more brandy. He had a look on his face like someone who'd been ambushed and was getting ready to lash out at his oppressors. "How be it if I take this back a ways to our splendid youth — no, let me be more precise, my brother here's splendid youth. He once knew this girl — a lovely girl, really — named Alice Harron."

To my surprise Clyde's spirit suddenly sagged. I could see it in his face. I could feel that his mind was now racing. "Um," he said and sat back down on the bed, splashing his drink onto his pants — which he brushed madly. A couple of nurses hurried by the door, and we all glanced over.

"Come on," Pretti said. "Let's all hear about this Alice Harron."

"Well, OK, but it's not what you think, Eddie." He put his hand on his heart. "I swear, it's not."

He looked as sunken as Bunny had. "Eddie here was dating this girl named Alice who was having some trouble with her math."

"What?" I said.

"She was having some trouble with her math, I said. You had told her that I was some kind of math genius, so she looked me up in the book one day and called — just out of the blue like that. She said who she was and asked if I could help her with her math."

Now it was Clyde who was staring down into the drink in his lap.

"Well, you know how much I like helping people, Eddie, so I was unwilling to at first, but she begged me. She said she was calling because you had said it was OK, but you wouldn't call *for* her."

"You *didn't*."

"I told you. It was all innocent, I swear."

"You were already married."

"What?" Pretti said, huffing. "Is that true?"

"Well, yes, it's true, but — well, I'll come back to that, possibly." His face shone red as an apple. "Anyway, Eddie, I didn't have to tell this story, but I'm telling it, OK?"

"OK, *tell it already*," I said.

"So what I was going to say was that she asked me to help her with her math, and I thought — what the heck? — what harm can come of it? But we meet in this restaurant near my office one day and, boy, she wasn't bad, Eddie, and, anyway, I'm innocently opening her math book to the chapter she was telling me about, she's sitting right beside me quite close, and she starts jamming her boobs into me — first one, then, in case I missed it, the other one comes swishing by." Clyde looked ragged as he spoke. I could see beads of perspiration forming on his upper lip. Clapping his drink with his free hand and splashing it again, he slipped off the bed and stood near it, looking away from me at the window. "Anyway, the day she phoned you to call off the relationship, I was the one who made her do it."

"You were the one."

"I was the one. There — it's out in the open now. I was right there with her, and there was no one else there. Her parents were away someplace. I told her I couldn't stand doing what we were doing unless she came clean with you, and —"

"And so she called me. You had her tell me about Jesus making a special appearance to warn her about me, and you just sat there."

202

"I didn't tell her to say that! It was finished between the two of you anyway — can't you understand that? Eddie, I swear, this has not been an easy thing for me. I was there, yes, and stark naked to boot, but I couldn't bring myself to perform though she worked those fine boobs of hers and that mouth. I —"

"Spare us the details, please. I can imagine."

"Eddie, I can't tell you how sorry I am, I really can't. This has been eating away at me for a long time now. What else can I say?"

I sat there, glowering at him, feeling as if I'd taken an immense blow to the gut, not once looking over at Bunny on one side or Pretti on the other. I felt the shoal of tears swimming to the surface yet again; then just as quickly they headed off in another direction. A second later, I cracked up. It took me and everyone else by surprise, I'm sure. Pretti got to her feet while I was still cackling like a madman, and Bunny soon followed.

"And just when do you plan to tell Jane?" I finally said.

"Let's go," Pretti said.

I said, "Let me ask you a question, my dear brother, if I may. Why do you bring me with you to a place like this? Do you do it to torture me? Do you do it to torture yourself? Do you want me to witness you becoming the legend you think you are? Or is it that, without me, you think you might go too far? Is that what it is, you jerk?"

Clyde said nothing.

"You see," I went on, "I don't give a sweet damn that you slept with Alice. I might've at the time, Clyde, but I don't any more. All I care about is that you slept with Bunny — with *Bunny*, you moron!"

"Who's Clyde?" Pretti said.

"What are you talking about?" Clyde said. Now he was on his feet, looming over me. "What the hell's Bunny to you?"

Pretti was already at the door. "Are we *ready?*" she said to Bunny.

"Just about," Bunny said, but she paused one last time to listen.

"I asked you a question," Clyde said.

"What I was hoping you would tell us, *Bobby*, is how you slept with Bunny when I left her in our room — helpless, defenseless — in a goddamn *stupor*, for Christ's sake. That's when you took advantage of her after chickening out the night before."

"What?" Bunny said. "I'm outta here." And she was.

Pretti paused to look at Clyde. "You slept with *Bunny?*" Then she, too, was gone.

"You really are the king of all jerks, you know that?" Clyde said, stomping toward the door.

"Oh, give it a rest," I said, slamming my drink down, so that it splashed all over the bedside table. I heard the winds howling at the window again and wanted to howl right back at them.

I tied up my hospital gown and followed everyone else out. For whatever reason, I expected the three of them to be standing in the hall, conferring on our little game of Cringers, waiting for me to take my turn. I found only Clyde at the elevator, and when he saw me, he chose the stairs instead.

I felt a yearning for Bunny now that made my head pound. And then I heard a familiar voice coming from one of the rooms.

Chapter Fifteen

"I've learned two important things in life," the voice said. "One is that it is sometimes best and most reassuring to see things from a single angle, and the other is that it is sometimes better to study a battle from behind a big, old tree than it is to skip along into the middle of it."

"I'm sure I don't know what you mean."

I crept toward the open door from which the voices were coming. Inside were big Louis inside and Ezio — and *Almond*, in bed with a bandage around his head! Who could have done this to him — the highlanders?

"If someone asked me, what would you rather have — heating or air conditioning — I'd say heating if it was winter when I was being asked. Do you follow me, Almon'? If it was summer and I could draw back and contemplate my survival, not my comfort, I might still say heating because you can survive a steamy day without air conditioning but not a frigid one too long without heating."

"I don't know what the hell you're talking about," Almond said.

"What I'm saying is that, if someone asked me what I'd rather keep, my sight or my hearin', I'd tell him it depends on what I was doing at the time. If I was listening to some beautiful music, I'd have my eyes closed and not care much about them — be ready to trade in anything to keep my ears — but if I was watching a beautiful woman sashay about, I'd want those eyes of mine to be sharp as a hawk's."

Almond looked calmer now, settling in for the ride.

Louis spoke quietly and slowly, as if in a confessional. "It seems to me," he said, "that you like to prevail over people when they don't have their eyes and ears working all at once. You're that sort of fellow — that's what I'm driving at. You don't contemplate all the angles, whether it's heating or air conditioning, or rather you put yourself in a position to be the *only* one contemplating all the angles. Do you catch my drift?"

"No, I don't," Almond said.

"We been hearing you been doing some unsavory tings to some visitor friends of ouahs," Ezio said, sitting on the bed and leaning heavily on Almond's chest, "and even woise to that little ex o' yoahs."

"What do you boys want from me?"

"Well, we fahgave da little debt o' yoahs we never mention any moah. You got some gamblin' problems and we got some solutions. Dey woiked once — we nevah come around to colleck da little debt — but now we want fo' you to keep youah little act clean. Am I comin' trough to yah?" Ezio was an inch from Almond's face. I could almost feel his breath on him. "You just stay behin' dat tree and outta da line o' fiah, my deah, and fahget about it ahready." Little Ezio pinched Almond's chin and shook his face. The tiny assailant stepped straight out of some forties gangster movie.

The two of them rose, Louis hoovering in a cloud of breath, and ambled out toward me. I stood to the side, hoping at first to escape, but holding my ground. "Well, look who's here," Louis said.

"I want to thank you gentleman for everything you've done," I whispered.

"What da hell happened to youah head? Fahget about it," Ezio said, pinching my chin and shaking my face.

"It wasn't Almonetti in there, was it, son?" Louis asked.

"No, sir. I walked into a lamppost."

The unlikely pair got their laugh of the evening just as a nurse approached from behind. "Well, well, gentlemen —" it was the unmistakable rasp of Brenda! Maybe my humble requests at The Way of Life Assembly of God Church had begun to pay off in spades. "Visiting hours are over. Maybe you can come by again tomorrow if that isn't too much trouble."

"None whatever, ma'am," Louis said, tipping a hat he wasn't wearing. Actually, a nice white Panama with a gold trim would have suited him fine just about then.

"You watch out for them lampposts," he said to me and winked before striding off with Ezio. "And, by the way," Louis said, turning back one last time, "little Kathleen has the address of that woman you were asking about."

"Oh, thanks. Thank her for me."

"No sweat," he said.

I was left to stand there with Brenda, her arms crossed, waiting for an explanation. She was even tapping her clumpy white nurse's shoe in my direction.

"I guess you're surprised to see me," I said.

"No, not as surprised as you are to see me, I'm sure. I was at the desk when your brother and his floozies brought you in."

I thought the floozies remark was uncalled-for, but under the circumstances I let it go.

"Do you have time to get a hot chocolate?" I asked.

"No, but where's your room? I have time for a little chat."

Brenda made herself comfortable in the chair Bunny had sat in while I creaked back onto my bed again. Brenda was looking around at the bottle and glasses. "I guess we had quite a howdown in here," she said.

"Just a friendly visit."

"I'll bet." Brenda's raspy voice was getting to me again, and my eyes began to well up. She gave me a good, hard look. I guess she took my tears to mean that I was wracked with guilt when in fact I was merely tugged by it.

"What happened to your head?" she asked. "Did you really walk into a lamp pole?"

"No. I got into a little scuffle — not long after I left your place, actually."

"Nemesis," she said.

"Whatever. Anyway, some guys wanted to steal my car —"

"So you fought them off for it?"

"Roughly speaking."

"That's too bad," Brenda said, "but tell me something." She pulled her chair closer to me by the bed. "Tell me about the girl you have back home."

Her voice was killing me. I wiped my eyes with the blanket. "I don't have a girl back home, Brenda. I'm sorry I misled you, but there's a girl here in Atlantic City, one of the floozies you referred to earlier, and —"

"You didn't mislead anyone," Brenda said, her voice

relaxing now. "We met in a late-night bar, you came up to my place for hot chocolate, then decided you weren't thirsty — no harm done."

"I'm sorry. I guess you wondered about it for a while."

"Not really. I didn't think it was the naval artifacts that scared you off. Look, people come and go in my life. It's par for the course."

"Well, I didn't so much come or go, Brenda, as stroll through it."

Brenda got to her feet. "Either way, it wouldn't have mattered much, would it? — Or it would have been worse. You'd have stayed with me last night and might even have stayed longer, kept in touch, something, and eventually you'd have taken off on me. It's better this way, believe me. Nothing much happened. *Really.* You are absolved." Brenda made the sign of a cross in the air over my bed.

Now that she'd said it, I couldn't have felt worse. If Desmond Pencil had wandered by the door just then, I'd have crushed Brenda against me and never let go.

"So what do you think?" I said. "Would you like to have one little dance before you go back to work."

"I don't think so, Eddie."

"One little dance won't hurt."

"All right, why not?" she said. "It's a quiet night. Why don't I just hum — how 'bout that?"

"Whatever," I said.

As lightly as a moth, Brenda fluttered to the door to lock it. She was already back when I switched off the bedside lamp to let the full moon work its cool but tender light through the window. Brenda put a light hand on my shoulder and nudged me backward as she began to hum the climactic aria from Puccini's *Madama Butterfly*. The sand-paper in her throat together with the faint, tragic notes of the song caused me to cry in earnest — but without my usual hyena sound effects — just quietly and wetly. How good things seemed for a moment, how warm the night and quiet the winds at the window. What a long, long day and night unraveled as we shuffled slowly around the hospital's linoleum floor, me in bare feet and Brenda with her nurse's shoes. Why hadn't Merv thought to install his glistening starlights in the ceiling here? He might even have persuaded the administration to have allowed him to throw in a couple of well-placed slot machines in the halls to lighten the suffering of the sick and weary by adding to the dings of the red alert a few clangs of good hope. Oh, *yes*, Miss America was born and bred right here in Atlantic City, and yes, Rudy Valee and his Connecticut Yankees had played to the throngs; yes, Marilyn Monroe *had* floated along its Boardwalk; and, yes, Mr. Planters Peanut doled out his free samples of Georgia warmth. We had it all and plenty to spare!

Brenda's cheek brushed against mine just as the tie of my gown fell open at the back, and my feet seized up on me. She stepped away, still humming, pulled off her little nurse beret, unbuttoned her top, her back now to me, swaying, sashaying like Marilyn, the loosened pins of her hair releasing the riot of honey curls around her thin but lively face, the shoes thudding off against the wall, the stockings rasping together in harmony with the gravely song now spewing somewhere from deep in her throat.

And then she turned, the buttons of her top now open to the waist. It was dark as I made my way to the bed and stretched out on its far side. Brenda snuggled in beside me and kissed my cheek. The light from the window etched a silver square over our forms. "Spread *out*," I kept wanting to tell it. "Wide angle." I allowed my hand to snake in under Brenda's white blouse until it encountered the soft-wheat texture of hair. My hand stopped, as though the message of the touch had scattered on its way to my brain. I moved the disembodied hand again slightly, the fingers combing through the quiet but insistent hairs.

The hand froze. Brenda froze.

"Does it bother you?" came that voice.

I hurtled over Brenda out of the bed. I stood looking down at her. She grinned in the dark. I took a gulp big enough to swallow a Buick. Brenda stood, too, careful not to touch me as she did, and began buttoning up. "I'm sorry," she said as she gathered up her shoes and bent over to slip them on. I heard the pattering of rain on the window.

"Brenda, it's not that I don't think you're a really nice guy. I'm the one who's sorry." Except for her hair and the little cap, she was ready to leave. I marveled as I watched her nimbly pin the whole thing together. "It must be difficult — I mean, here, or whatever."

"I guess it is," Brenda said. We'd gotten to the part where, hope against hope, Brenda could stop skulking in sad, gray locker rooms, dallying with a button, massaging a foot, waiting for the room to clear before she could change.

She kept her head down. It was as if a carnival spotlight had suddenly come on and she'd been found out to have been part of the spectacle, not the audience, not the passers-by.

She had managed to slip out of the circus tent past the sentries of Apple Pie America, and was now being marched right back in again.

I stretched forward, extending my neck like a crane, to plant a kiss on Brenda's cheek, feeling real affection through the tip of my beak.

"It's OK," she said. "Honest, it is. I hope you get that girl you were looking for."

As Brenda said this and blew me a kiss, a miracle came to pass: her voice no longer made me cry.

Chapter Sixteen

There was no hospital bill to pay the following morning when I checked out, and no one who could tell me whether it was Brenda or Clyde who had settled the account for me. Brenda was nowhere to be found. And Almond, too. I'd taken a great deal of care creeping over to his room only to find he had vanished and his bed had been made. I thought I might still have been dreaming and none of this had happened: not the Cringers, not Louis, not Brenda. Except that I was standing at the checkout desk of an Atlantic City hospital.

I was wearing my brother's herringbone, which he'd been kind enough to leave for me, and it came complete with my wallet, a hotel key, and in the same pocket, a Vitamin C tablet big enough to feed a nation. I popped the pill and took a cab back to the hotel, which turned out to be just around the corner from the hospital. I kept thinking on the way what exactly I could say to Bunny. Memories of the night before pounded through my head.

At the Resorts, there was no sign of life in the room, and no message had been left for me at the desk. I took a cursory survey of the blackjack and craps tables in the casino. No one. I started to feel anxious again and abandoned. I scooted over to the Taj Mahal. Before the

Alhambra Room stood a larger-than-life, colorful card with a big, bad image of a chubby face and the caption, "WAYNE NEWTON! TWO NIGHTS ONLY!" There was no message left for me at the Taj Mahal, and Bunny had checked out. Pretti hadn't, but she was not answering the phone in her room.

Back in my room, I took a baby bottle of Chivas from the mini-bar and an Almond Joy and sat down to wait. I knew one thing already. I knew that I could never have done what Clyde had done with Alice, but I also believed that, even if I *had* done it, I would not have been able to tell anyone.

But how could Clyde have lived so long with that little morsel wedged in his throat? If discretion was the better part of valor, the rest was duplicity. Some hidden but significant part of courage, I now knew, had to do with living a double life. Some people were very good at leading double and even triple lives. Some were hardly good at leading even a single life. Clyde and my father belonged to the first category, my mother and I, to the second. When he was forty, my father bought some small apartment buildings in partnership with an old Swiss friend of his. All the two of them had to do to stay afloat was pick up the rents at the end of each month and call in a plumber or electrician every once in a while. But somehow my father managed to turn the job into something much bigger. He bought himself a nice, leather attaché case, stuffed a few sheets of paper in it along with a bank book and headed out the door each morning at nine. He often didn't make it home until minutes before the dinner gong at six. I tried to imagine where he'd wandered: the bridge club, probably, as a start, one of the many restaurants around town as a follow-up, a matinée feature now and again. When we went out to dinner as a family, he always had a new place for us to go, together with a review of what was best on the menu. Friends of mine occasionally reported seeing him coming out of strange doors on streets he had no business being on. Or they'd run into him in front of the stock exchange, reading the electronic ticker tape.

The key to this system, though, was that we did not talk about these things. I had been into that attaché case of his at the end of the day and seen nothing at all. *I* knew he had not been out conducting business. My mother knew. Clyde knew. Even Jane and Alice Harron knew, for God's sake. But nothing was ever said. It was an arrangement we all had. There was food on the table, clothing on our backs, a roof over our heads, and a family living its life, so there was little we could say if we wanted to keep the boat afloat. And the advantage to us young'uns was that Clyde and I were also never to be asked where *we* were going when we went out. That was also part of the deal. Even when I offered to tell, my father would hold up his hand and say, "That's your business. I'm sure you'll be fine." (My mother, meanwhile, wanted to know and tried to find out whenever she could — quietly, off to the side or in the kitchen.)

And that was the system Clyde adopted for himself when he started his family. If Jane didn't already know he led a double life, she certainly sensed it, and on balance decided it wasn't worth asking about. The partner of a person leading a double life has to have a double consciousness, which consists of knowing some things and steering clear of others.

I've met whole families who have lived this way. A friend of mine in junior high, Jerry Lawson, smoked a pack of cigarettes a day, but he was not allowed to do so at home because both his parents were not only ex-smokers, but they'd also become militant *anti*-smokers. The whole family, though, had a secret drawer in an old dresser in the basement, and there was always a carton of cigarettes in there which they *all* smoked on the sly — Jerry, the militant ex-smoking parents, Jerry's friends, the parents' friends — and always, when the carton ran out, a new one would materialize. Still, no one smoked officially, and all the Lawsons sat around after dinner, craving the old weed and wishing everyone else would get lost so they could sneak down to the basement for a puff.

I didn't believe it at the time, but I now think that it was brave of my father and now Clyde to go ahead and live their second lives, whatever they were. Better that than to fester away, wanting something they didn't have, feeling the thick, green, bitter blood flowing through their veins. Follow your heart and keep it to yourself. That way not that many dreams get shattered. Then, at a ripe moment, you can even add discretion to your Hall of Valor by coughing up a nugget from your double life right onto the floor of your single life, the way Clyde did with the Alice Harron cringer, and look noble as you seek forgiveness. If you let it, the whole thing can make you sick because you have to have a double life in the first place even to play the game.

So it dawned on me then, in that chair at the Resorts, with our million-dollar curtains thrown wide open, that I was brought here just to see it all happen — single-lived Eddie

Markson, along to watch a chapter of his brother's double life unfold, merely riding the running board of Clyde's brazen second self.

I took a hearty swig from the little bottle and threw my head back. I felt kind of old and got myself a preview of what it would be like to spend my remaining years in a chair. I wondered what Brenda was up to and what I'd have done if, that first night, I'd waited long enough for her to come out of the bathroom dressed only in his or her gotchies. What was she thinking in the night as she went about her business, getting set to go to bed, stripping off the uncomfortable gear of the other gender, peeling the white stockings off her stubbly legs, humming *M. Butterfly* as she hung them over her radiator and peered out the window at the City of Shattered Glass? What could I have done so as not to have offended her back in that dark hospital room?

The Almond Joy — just two bites of it, actually — began to repeat on me, and I slipped into an Almond Sadness that for the moment seemed bottomless. Before long, I fell into a dreamless sleep in my jacket in the chair.

It was already three in the afternoon when I got up. For whatever reason, I felt a renewed vigor. I straightened myself out in the bathroom mirror, trying to comb my hair down to cover the bump on my forehead, which had shrunk but still shined like the tub it had come up against.

By some coincidence, the same cab and driver who had brought me back from the hospital was parked right in front of the hotel. I hoped he'd had another run or two in between but decided he didn't look cheerful enough for me to inquire about it. I got in and asked if he knew of an elementary school with a soldier out front who might have been holding a bayonet.

"Martin Luther King, Jr. Elementary and Middle," he piped right up.

"Can you get me there in kind of a hurry?"

He nodded and had us up on Atlantic before I'd had time to sit back. It took only a few more minutes to get to the school. I could see from a distance that a security guard stood out front, but he was holding some kind of machine gun, not a bayonet. I paid and headed straight for the guard, nodding hello and smiling as I walked around the front of the school to the side where in fact there was a soldier with a bayonet as Kathleen had described it, but he was a statue. He stood over the bank, his rifle pointing out at the murky canal. The inscription at the base read, *"To Our Proud Civil War Dead, 1861–1865 AD. Behold This Stone Shall Be a Witness Unto Us."*

The entrances to the school around the side and back were all locked. I trotted around to the front again, tipped an imaginary hat to the guard the way big Louis would have done, and said, "I'm here to pick up my niece." I opened my jacket wide. "I'm not packing heat or anything, no need to sound the alarm."

The guy narrowed his eyes at me as he had every right to do. I slid past him, through the door and rushed down the big, granite-floored hall, never once looking back. I could tell I was in the elementary wing from the pictures decorating the walls: bright suns with their bright sun eyelashes, tilting houses and fat, colorful flowers as big as the people sprinkling them. There was one picture, though — there's always one — signed by "Meereeam B." (was that her parents' spelling or hers?) — whose sad portrait of a young black girl looked out at us with black, sad eyes. There was a glint of light in the irises exactly where a glint of light needed to appear, and with the tight little pigtails tied with red ribbons and curled upward and outward from the drooped, brown face — stood out like the work of a modern-day Rembrandt.

What I would have given then to have photographed the watercolor and blown it up for my own wall. If it hadn't belonged to a child, I would have stolen the piece right there and then. I made a mental note to keep my eyes on the career of young Meereeam B-something.

Further down the hall were glass cases filled with sewing and crude wooden clocks with tin numbers. I knew now that I was getting warm and began peering in the windows of one classroom after another, looking for Kathleen, staying at each window for as long as it took for a kid to notice me and start pointing or, in one case, for the teacher herself to have a suspicious look over.

And then I came to a door, Room 17, the second-to-last room on the corridor, and spotted Kathleen immediately, sitting prim and attentive in the front row. She, too, saw me quickly enough, along with a half dozen other kids, and I was just trying to come up with some kind of signal to let her know I was waiting for her when a meaty hand landed on my shoulder from behind. I turned to find what looked like the principal with his pal, the security guard, packing the heavy artillery.

"I'm Mr. Brown," the principal said. "Can I help you in some way?"

"Oh, not really. I'm Mr. Markson. I'm just here to

pick up my niece, Kathleen."

Mr. Brown looked in the window, and Kathleen waved, much to my relief. "Mr. Markson, most of our children take the school bus home." The principal was speaking just above a whisper. "It's rather unusual to have someone here, prowling the halls, waiting for children. Most relatives wait in their cars out front."

"Well, I thought I'd surprise her, that's all. No big deal. Just a surprise, really — I'm from out of town."

"Does Kathleen's mother know that you're here?"

"Nope, a surprise there, too."

"Are you her half-brother, perhaps?"

"Adopted."

The security guard was smiling now, running his chin along the barrel of his gun.

"You don't mind if we check these things out. Do you, Mr. Markson?"

"Not in the slightest. Why should I mind?"

Mr. Brown dismissed the smiling security guard, and I followed the principal's big, soft shoes around the corner toward his office. He paused to look in on the janitor in a little cubby hole. The janitor had great big droopy eyes with irises that shone crimson in the half light, like two vanilla cones pointed toward us with cherries on top.

"Samuel, you won't forget about those tar markings on the back wall." Samuel shook his head. "They're pretty bad," the principal said.

"I won't forget." I heard some faint clanging and then some muffled applause as Samuel turned toward a small black-and-white TV set behind the door. He was watching *The Price is Right*, and nothing about it seemed out of place for me. What I mean is that this was the place, this country, and the only place for *The Price is Right* and for *All in the Family* and *Barnaby Jones*. I felt suddenly drawn toward the scene as if I belonged to it. For my whole life I'd been watching these shows from over a fence, awaiting the stars' approval — waiting for just a nod in our direction — to hear them say they were running away to Canada — but it was here they truly belonged, here where the price was truly right and all the shows were true. This was the land of Bob Barker and Andy Griffith and big Louis and Almonetti, and no matter how lousy or hokey it all was, they were proud always to wear their silly hearts on their sleeves because they beat as sure as all America. My own heart felt an idiotic surge of patriotism, a stirring in my gut that told me this where it was all happening, here and in Topeka and Lake Tahoe, and if you were not here, you were not anywhere. Even *I* had been here long enough now that I was ready to pledge allegiance at the drop of a hat.

Samuel went back to gazing at his little silver screen, and we continued along to the principal's office where, crossed over the doorway, hung two great, heartfelt flags, one for the United States and the other for the State of New Jersey to welcome its newest citizen.

"I'll only be a minute," Mr. Brown said to his secretary. "Can you bring me the number of Kathleen Danso, please?"

Danso? What kind of name was that, I wondered? While we waited, Mr. Brown made a whistling motion with his lips, but no sound came out. He had opera playing in the background, coming from a radio I couldn't see anywhere. The music was my favorite aria: the duet of the two friends from *The Pearl Fisher*. I felt at ease right away, even a kind of kinship, a feeling I now added to my patriotism.

I was grateful, all the same, when the school bell rang. The phone number was brought, and Mr. Brown squinted as he looked at the piece of paper and dialed. When he finished, he swung around away from me, but swung right back again. "The line is busy." He dialed and hung up again. As we waited, he picked up a couple of letters he'd obviously read before and looked them over again. Then he dialed again, drumming the desktop with the fingers of his other hand, took a strange look at the receiver and hung up. There was a photograph on the wall of a girl in graduation gear and beside it another one of the same girl talking to a horse, it looked like. "Do you know —" he said just as Kathleen came bounding through the door.

"Here's my niece now," I said, getting to my feet.

"Uncle Eddie," Kathleen said, taking my elbow.

"Under normal circumstances," Mr. Brown said, "I would not allow one of my children to make off with a stranger, you understand."

"Absolutely," I said, "and I appreciate your taking such care with my niece and her schoolmates."

"All right then," he said and waved us on.

On the way to her locker, Kathleen asked me what had happened to my head. I told her I'd had a little tangle with a wild gambler who didn't take very well to losing.

We had to stop at her locker on the way out and, as it turned out, had to discuss a geography assignment with another girl who refused to understand what Kathleen was talking about.

When we finally made it outside, there was a great deal of commotion and a swarm of young boys around the Civil

War memorial. The security guard was by the door, paying no attention whatever. "Oh, no," Kathleen said as I smiled at the guard and stepped down. "They do this practically every day. It's really stupid. They try to knock over the statue, and a whole bunch of the goofs get into the act." I stopped at the foot of the stairs while Kathleen stayed at the top, shielding her eyes from the sun.

The security guard asked her to move along home. She turned and looked at him down the barrel of her eyes. "You are not the boss of me," she said, then planted her feet as she looked over at the trouble. "Oh, no," she said again. "Those Barker boys are here again. They don't even go to this school. They don't go to *any* school." She turned to the security guard. "The *Barker* boys are here again." The guard looked but didn't move. He rubbed the wooden stalk of his gun.

"Let's go," I said to Kathleen. "We should go." But she wouldn't budge.

A great cry rose from the throngs just as Mr. Brown's car swooped around the building and edged forward through the crowd. His car window was open, and I could hear the same tenor duet from *The Pearl Fisher* I'd heard inside. He must have taken the tape with him.

"Oh, no," Kathleen squealed this time. The security guard walked slowly down the stairs and off in the direction of the car. I could see the Yankee's bronze head move and the tip of the bayonet quiver. Kathleen looked at me pleadingly, and I followed the security guard. Samuel, the janitor, was right behind me, looking a little shopworn and dejected. We waded right in through the mêlée, though by nature I am not a cheerful mêlée-wader, and I noticed up ahead that the principal's car door had been thrown wide open, Bizet's pearl fisher calling out to the bright blue heavens, and Brown was doing the very thing I'm sure principals complain about most when they get together in some out-of-the-way Holiday Inn once a year to discuss their lives and salaries and whether or not all of this was really worth it at the end of the day: he marched straight toward the statue, clearing the crowds like Moses as he went, and ordered everyone, Barker boys included, to leave the statue alone, please. He then fell out of view, though I could still hear his shrill voice above that of the boys, "*Leave* the damn statue *alone, please.*"

I let Samuel outpace me. I reminded myself that I'd come here, after all, just to get Bunny's address. What's more, there was a tendency, I quickly noted, once ungovernable impulses got the better of a crowd, for the impulses to heat up until they boiled over in a crisis. And there I was, the glacier of sobriety, inching forward to do — what? Knock over the ineducable Barker boys?

I checked back over my shoulder only to see Kathleen jumping up and down even more excitedly. When I turned back, the unthinkable was happening: Mr. Brown had been hoisted up above the crowd and was now being held precariously over the lifeless soldier's bayonet. I'd lost sight of the guard, and then to my horror, I saw Samuel a few thick paces ahead crouch to help the fallen man as so many tiny feet stomped all around and over him.

"Eddieeee!" I thought I heard Kathleen cry out, but when I turned I could no longer see her. A bolt of panic shot through me. What had happened to little Kathleen? I had nearly made it to the car; Luciano and his pal had finished their aria; the car itself was rocking; and I turned again, thinking Kathleen might have been trying to find me; passed Samuel who'd helped the guard back to a sitting position; and drew closer, the only adult left except for Brown himself who, despite his precarious position up there in the air, looked more exasperated than terrified. I rose up tall and blew out my chest like a bullfrog and opened my mouth to shout a stop to all of this, but a car horn blasted out instead. It was Kathleen in the driver's seat! Trailing out of the blast, machine gun bullets pocked the air and quieted the crowd, and then came the choking smell of smoke. Brown sank below eyeshot. I broke through and saw him lying on the ground before the unmoved soldier. Brown was wiping his pate with a handkerchief. In the distance, I spotted what must have been the three Barker boys hightailing it out of there along the canal; the younger tough boys scattered; then the car horn rang out again.

I worked my way through this animated movie over to the car again, got Kathleen by the hand — she had her homework on the other seat, for God's sake, and took hold of it — before I could haul her out and away from her elementary schoolmates.

A frantic minute or two later, we were in a cab, Kathleen and I — the *same cab, same driver* I'd come with — and, of all things, we were giggling our way along Atlantic toward Ventnor. "Troy Avenue," Kathleen, still laughing, told the driver. He nodded, his face lifeless as always, and had us roaring along.

There was a coffee shop a few blocks up, and I asked the driver to pull over and wait, "unless you get another fare, of course," I added, and he rolled his eyes. The place was called "Coffee and Things." Kathleen stepped in, marched right up to the counter and said, "We'd like coffee and 12 or 13 things" and broke into a new round of laughter. The guy at the cash register turned and walked through a swinging steel door. Maybe he'd heard this one before. Kathleen had not forgotten to bring her small knapsack filled with homework and made herself comfortable in a booth.

"Do you really want coffee?" I asked her.

"No, maybe a soda," she said, catching her breath after all the laughter. "A root beer, maybe, and could I have a chocolate éclair, do you think?"

"Of course." I sauntered over to the counter, my knees still jittery from our little episode back at the school, and waited with my money out for the Coffee and Things man to come back through the swinging door. That poor Brown back there at the school. He'd obviously spent his life trying to maintain law and order — he gave *me* the once over, for cripe's sakes — and here he was with statue-topplers to contend with at the end of each day.

It took me a while to get back to our booth with our order. I got coffee and a cinnamon cruller, which on first bite tasted more like a big, old hunk of bread than anything else, but the coffee was quite good and hit the spot.

I said, "I understand you found out where Bunny Tremaine lives."

"Yep," Kathleen chirped, licking éclair cream off her thumb and holding on to the secret a moment longer. "She lives way over in Longport, on 12th, near the Egg Harbor side."

"Egg Harbor?"

"Yep. My mom said it's where this bar of land narrows. It's Bunny's mom and sister that live there, actually, in a small house. They're called the Lopezes, though, not the Bunny Tremaines."

"Can we get there along this route?"

"Yep, I think so. It's 106 — 12th Avenue. We'll just tell the driver."

"I don't think that's a good idea — you coming along with me, I mean. We can drop you off on the way there."

"You can drop me on the way back, too."

"That's true, but I have a kind of serious matter to settle there, and I should probably do it on my own. Besides, your mother will be worried about you, and we probably can't reach her by phone."

Kathleen's eyes drooped as she continued to chomp down on the creamy éclair. There was no one else in the coffee shop this time of day, though the place was nice and clean, had fresh coffee and what seemed like an upstanding proprietor though I could not be sure of anything anymore.

"Is she your sweety?" Kathleen said, her eyes now bright and smiling.

"No, I wouldn't call her that."

She slurped her root beer, and I shoved my cruller aside. "Are you married?" she asked. "Do you have kids?"

"No. And no."

"Oh. . . . That's interesting." Kathleen gave the word all of its syllables. "My school's pretty jumpy, huh?" she said.

"It sure is. Does that kind of thing go on every day?"

"No, you got lucky, but it *is* real jumpy a lot of the time."

Kathleen sighed through a last, tired chew.

"Why do you think those kids did that?" I asked. Kathleen shrugged her shoulders. Her bones were as slender as a bird's. "I mean, why do you suppose that kind of thing goes on?"

"I don't know," she said, sighing again, and resting her face in the cup of her hands.

"Is it boredom? Are they bored?"

"Yep, I guess."

"Are they bored and unhappy?"

She lifted her face out of her hands and looked me dead in the eyes. "Why do you sound like a TV reporter?" she asked. "I think you sound like a TV reporter."

"I'm sorry. I didn't mean to."

Kathleen poked through the ice cubes in her glass with her straw, slurping the brown remnants of her root beer. The taxi driver was still sitting outside our window, never once looking over at us, smoking a slow cigarette. There were some bright, little businesses on the other side of the street, one selling lace things, it looked like, but they didn't look very active. They were as still and quiet as an Edward Hopper painting.

"Would you like another éclair?" I asked.

"No, thank you." She was looking out the window. "Do you know," she continued, "that this is not a safe place for you — Atlantic City, I mean."

She killed me. "It's not safe for *me?* What about you?"

"I know my way around here. But I think someone like you could get hurt in a place like this. I like having you here, but I don't think it's safe."

I looked into her serious eyes and decided to move on.

"Maybe you're right, Kathleen." She seemed old to me suddenly.

"You know," I said, "that I have a brother, named Clyde, who talked me into coming down here, and until this very moment I couldn't understand why, exactly. It's because he fits in here with the Clint Eastwoods and Al Capones and Miss Americas. Maybe there's more excitement — or more anger — or maybe you're just allowed to express it here, I don't know. But people think that losing their temper and reaching for the nearest guns and lances and Civil War monuments makes them bigger — like an explosion. But I think the opposite is true. Instead of becoming big like their shouting voices, they shrink — as if firing their cannons makes them one cannonball lighter. Do you know what I mean?"

"I don't think so," Kathleen said.

"I mean, it's like what Louis said about the angle from which you look at things."

"Who's Louis?"

"Oh, no one. What I mean is that anger doesn't make you bigger; it diminishes you. It makes people smaller and smaller with each explosion, until they're battling among the weeds and candy wrappers and field mice. Their eyes may get beadier. They may get redder and hotter and puff themselves up, but their egos won't grow an inch. You know, just when you think you're becoming King Kong, you look in the mirror one day and see Jiminy Cricket. And so *that's* what it is. Clyde may actually keep me along because he looks *up* to me — if that's possible?"

Kathleen said, "What do you think Clyde would say about that?"

"*Clyde*? How do you mean?"

"Do you think he'd say you were right?"

"No, he never would."

"Do you think you're saying these things about my city," she pressed on, "to make *your*self feel better? Don't you think we're *all* that way, at least a bit — Clyde and you and me and your friend Louis, just a bit?" Kathleen looked down at the table at some crumbs. She might have been getting set to cry.

"Kathleen. I think you're smarter than I am. That's what I think. Your being here is not your fault, and I'm sorry — I didn't mean that. I meant —" and I suddenly wasn't sure what I'd meant. She *was* smarter than I was by a long shot.

"Do you know," I said, "I saw some Canada Geese out on the shore the other night?"

"*Where?*" Her face brightened.

"Near the hotels. Just wandering around, taking a little breather, I guess, on their way south."

"Oh, I *love* them. They hardly *ever* come through here. I love it when they do. They sometimes land on the bank near the soldier at school. I've only ever seen them once — *twice*, if you count the time out of our classroom window. Mrs. Blendern let us all leave our seats to look. Then, I saved part of my sandwich at lunch and ran out to see if I could give them some, but they were gone. I just *wish* I could've given them my sandwich."

"Well, if you come visit Canada sometime, you'll have a chance to see some geese. I'll take you out to a park where they live, and you can feed them a whole loaf of bread if you want to."

"I won't visit Canada."

"You won't?"

"I don't see how. Do you?"

"Why not? When it's vacation time sometime soon, you'll say, 'Why don't we visit Canada?' I came down *here* with my brother for no good reason at all."

Kathleen's mahogany eyes filled with possibility. After a moment she said, "Do you know that peacocks don't lay eggs?"

I was draining my coffee cup. "No, I didn't know."

"Yep. They're birds, but they don't lay eggs — isn't that strange? — or maybe it's just that they don't lay them in the usual way, I can't remember."

I looked out the window at our taxi driver and saw for the first time how high his cheekbones were. With the strong shadows, they looked like small platforms.

"That *is* strange," I said. "Are you sure?"

"Well, our teacher said they don't have their babies in the same way as other birds, exactly."

"What do they do, then? They can't have their young live. Only mammals do that."

"I don't know what they do. I'll know tomorrow, in science. We just got to how they make their babies strangely, so I was wondering how they do it when the bell rang."

"That has got to be the strangest animal on earth," I said.

"Maybe that's what it's trying to tell us by not laying eggs," Kathleen said. "Maybe it's trying to say that it's not like the other birds."

What I would have given just then to spirit Kathleen away to Jeffy's place, maybe, in his room with Ricky, his hamster, set her up with some big, round balls of snow out back and some buttons and sticks, so they could build a snowman. Or maybe she was too old for snowmen.

"I'm going to have to go soon," I said.

"Won't you take me with you?"

"I can't, Kathleen."

"Then, that's it, then," she said, stricken. "I won't ever come to Canada, maybe, probably, and you won't ever come back here because you were out late at night by yourself all wet and because you saw those boys try to hurt Mr. Brown."

"I *will* be back, and you *will* come visit sometime. Maybe not in the next few weeks, but *sometime*."

"Can I write to you?"

"I would love that," I said. Kathleen smiled a tiny smile, and I had a quick change of heart. "Isn't your mother going to mind if you come with me?" Her smile widened. "Isn't she going to worry where you got to after school?"

"No, she won't — honest. Lots of times I go to my friend Sylvie's after school for a little while. She won't mind, I swear.

"OK, but I want you to hang back in the car while I go up to Bunny's place."

"OK."

"I'll call out to you only if I need protection, OK?"

She laughed wildly.

Leo Bulmer once told me that this old widower uncle of his from Poland had said at dinner that friends are infinitely replaceable. Leo and I talked about that when he told it to me one summer evening as we sat on a curb and smoked a cigarette he'd stolen from his mother. "It means, you're going to split in a few years, and I'll have someone else to hang around with all the time, and you'll have someone else, then *they'll* be gone, too, and we'll have someone else again." Still, I thought right then and told Leo that, even if that *did* happen, though I doubted it did, but even if it *did*, there were certain people you'd have to carry along with you for a very long time even if they'd moved to Borneo, stopped writing letters and had been burned at the stake.

That was the way I felt just then with little Kathleen sitting across from me and a cab driver with platformed cheeks waiting outside the window. As the grand avenue of my life shortened, suddenly, before my eyes, I knew that this young girl would be there at its end, as young as today, waving me on. I can be the corniest guy on earth, I swear, but these pictures I get in my mind choke me up every single time without fail. I sometimes feel like an old, round mountain, waiting for the day I'll finally level out with the rest of the land.

"Do you want to check out the geese first — see if they're down by the water now?" I said.

"Do you *mean* it?"

"Sure, why not? A few extra minutes won't make a difference. But we'll have to get them something to nibble on."

"Oh, this is wonderful!" Kathleen said, slapping her hands together, then gathering up her knapsack.

I bought two lumpy crullers, one orange and one cherry, which looked as though they were getting ready for the birds anyway, and a coffee for our driver. In the car, I asked our man to take us to the boardwalk and wait.

He dropped us off at a nearby stretch of the wooden walk which I didn't recognize, and there wasn't a bird to be seen — nor even a human. I could just make out the hotels in the distant mist.

"Where are they?" Kathleen said, stepping off the planks and plopping herself down in the sand. "Where do you suppose they are?"

"I don't know. I don't see them anywhere."

"Do you think they're off making babies?" she asked seriously.

"No, they're not like peacocks, I don't think. It could be they're afraid, that's all. Why don't we scatter the crullers anyway and see if they swoop in?"

Kathleen cheered to this suggestion and got to work immediately, crumbling the pastries in her little palms and running up and down the beach, scattering lines of them all the way back to me. She resumed her seat, and we quietly studied the lines, like Hansel and Gretel.

Kathleen spotted a yogurt tub nearby, got up to fill it with ocean water and began to make mud pies by my feet. As she sat on her haunches, she looked even smaller and younger than she was.

The horn blast of a distant ship rang around the bay. And suddenly all the clichés were true — the gleaming sea, the sparkling sun — if only we could stay like this forever. If only night refused to fall, and the geese took their time and the cow jumped over the moon. We couldn't leave just yet. I didn't want to part company with this young girl. I wanted to pack her up and take her with me wherever I went. I wanted to take her to a five-year-long performance of *La Bohème*. I wanted to take her ice skating on a pond. I wanted her beside me on the couch, gawking at Brenda's navy paraphernalia. I wanted to feed her soggy fries at Barclay's and spirit her off to a funeral in North Carolina. If only she could see Glad and Sad in their twin track suits and sip NyQuil and play "Early One Morning" for them on her recorder, possibly, and eat Oh Henry bars with me, how much rosier life would be!

I felt a nip on my cheeks and realized they were damp. I was dabbing my eyes with my sleeve when Kathleen yelled, "Look!" She was pointing heavenward. "Look!"

There, above us, in a great and perfect V flew the Canada Geese, clattering and honking like Sunday picnickers.

"Down here!" Kathleen screamed. She picked up a few of the cruller crumbs she'd scattered and hurled them high. "Heeeere!"

I joined Kathleen and put my hand on her shoulder. "It's OK, Kathleen. They'll come back later for sure — around dinner time, most likely."

"No, they won't!" She was inconsolable. "They never will. They're on their way south. They'll end up in Florida and never pass this way again."

"Of course they will," I said but I too believed suddenly that they wouldn't. "They're just circling the bay to get some exercise," I said. "Look at that perfect V-formation. They're just showing off."

"They're not, Eddie. They're headed south. Did you see that leader in front? She knows what she's doing."

"Well, then, they'll be back next year at the latest."

"What if they're not? What if they've decided this is not a good place to stop; what if they never come back?"

"Because they know where they're going — that's what

you just said, isn't it? They have their spots picked out forever — that's what they *do*. Birds are great that way — and whales — and butterflies. The Monarch butterfly ends up in Monarch, California, every single year. Can you beat that?"

"No," she said, "but you can never be sure of anything." Her lips began to quiver.

I sank to my knees in the sand, hugged Kathleen and cried myself for about the forty-seventh time that day. I made a mental note to tell my friends that, if they ever wanted a really good sob, forget *Gone with the Wind* — visit Atlantic City.

Kathleen and I stayed there like that for a good long while, babbling and sniffling like a pair of giglets sitting in the principal's office awaiting punishment.

"Why don't we hang on a bit longer?" I said when Kathleen pulled away. "You never know. They may be back."

"OK," she said forlornly, but she soon spotted a flat stick and resumed baking her mud pies.

I sat back down on the edge of the boardwalk with my feet in the sand. I started flinging sand as far as I could with the toe of my shoe and beginning to feel I could challenge Clyde. The wind picked up some of the sand and rained it down on Kathleen. She giggled again and it warmed my heart. It was then, just as I was studying the clever little ledge at the toe of my shoe and getting in a really good dig, that I spotted a shiny object nearly a foot below the surface. It was a ring!

I scrambled to my knees to sift it out. "Kathleen!" I called out. "Look what I found!" She was looking straight up at the sky again. "No, here." It looked like a diamond engagement ring — and a good-sized diamond at that.

Kathleen took it from me gingerly, ran to the water to wash it, and I followed, delighted that I could surprise her. Kathleen held the ring up to the sun and squinted as she watched the gold glitter and the gem scatter light.

"I wonder how old it is," I said, "and which poor sap lost it."

Kathleen read the inscription in the interior of the band. "Charlie," she said. "It doesn't say anything else, just Charlie."

"Wow," I said. "Charlie. I bet his poor fiancée was sorry about losing the ring Charlie got her — for a pretty penny, too, I bet."

"Yeah." Kathleen rolled the ring around in her palm. She was getting sad again.

"You can have it, Kathleen. It's yours. You can hold onto it, or you can sell it if you want. That Cash for Gold guy at your place would give you a small fortune for it, I'm sure, and you can put the money into the bank for college."

"Charlie's girl didn't lose this," she said. She was still glum. "She threw it at him, probably, and they likely found other people to marry later on."

"Now, how can you possibly know that?" I asked.

"Because you don't lose a ring like this, Eddie. You'd be sitting on the beach all day long admiring it and showing it off. You throw a ring like this — you don't lose it. You throw it at Charlie, and then you have a fight, and then it's gone. You storm off, and then it's lost until it turns up years and years and years later when you're old, and when you've had a bad time maybe, and when you're feeling

237

sorry about the day you spent at Chicken Bone Beach."

"Is that what this is called, Chicken Bone Beach?" I asked.

"I don't know," she said, "but that's where the black folks had to have their holiday in Lannic City, Chicken Bone Beach."

"Oh," I said. I wondered about Kathleen's parents and gazed at her cheerfully as she went on studying the ring. It had an intricate floral pattern carved into the sides like a small garden.

"I'd better go," Kathleen said, brushing the sand off her knees. She was at least twice as smart at her tender age as I would ever be. "Maybe you'd better take me home now, Eddie."

"Are you sure?"

"Yes, I am. And maybe you should have the ring — you found it — it's only fair." She looked up at me and squinted.

"No way," I said. "It's yours for keeps."

She did not try it on, but zipped it into her pencil case in her knapsack. In the cab, we didn't exchange another word.

When we dropped Kathleen off at home, the place looked as welcoming as if I'd visited every day. The events of the night before seemed as if they had happened long in the past. I'd written my address out on a scrap of paper I'd found on the seat of the cab, and Kathleen now folded it gingerly and placed it, too, inside the secret pocket of her knapsack with her pencil case. Then flung her arms around my neck, as if she were sending me off to war.

"Bye," she said and was gone. I was the one left to stand

on the sidewalk to gaze at the closed door. The late autumn light was failing. I wondered for a second whether I shouldn't drop in to say hello to Lou, but was sure they'd all had enough of me. To be honest, *I'd* had enough of me, so why wouldn't they? I waited until what looked like a lantern was lit in the window of what must have been Kathleen's bedroom. And I was on my way again.

Chapter Seventeen

We zipped along to Longport, which took no time to get to, it seemed, and I became filled with apprehension over what it was, exactly, that I could say to Bunny. She seemed now like a distant dream to me, an apparition. For a moment, I had the sickening feeling — and it made me light-headed — that there was really nothing I had to offer her. She was better off with the imaginary Franks, conjured up by Almonetti, or with the Clydes of the world, people inhaling excitement from the very air they breathed, people electrified by every shadow and laneway, people who slithered down high school halls and were able to say with a straight face, "Hey, baby, you're for me," people who stood in the faces of giants and told them to back off.

Why would I want to make anyone miserable? How long would it be before Bunny read *The Red Badge of Courage* willingly?

Then that look of hers came into view, that look at the beginning of passion or sympathy, whatever it was, when her green eyes receded into the damp jungle shadows and anything was possible — likely even — where the greatest secrets in the world were stored, all barriers lifted, all sins absolved. Oh, what I would do to see that face across from me, now and again, ready to spring that look!

The cab driver pulled over beside the tiniest of houses and asked if I wanted him to wait. This time, I was the one rolling my eyes. An unlikely small, black sports coupe sat in the driveway — is *this* the kind of car Bunny drove? As I approached, I noticed the front door of the house was slightly ajar.

I took a couple of steps and froze. There was Bunny in front of me and the chiseled taxi driver behind. I looked back over my shoulder at the cab. I dropped to one knee on the lawn, put a hand over my heart, like Al Jolson, and sang,

> *That lucky old sun*
> *He's got nothin' to do*
> *But just roll around heaven all day.*

No, that was Ray Charles. No, I did not drop to one knee like Al Jolson to sing anything at all. I got scared instead. I scooted behind a huckleberry bush on the far side of the house and waited. I was panting when I peered through the thorny branches at my driver who sat unperturbed, smoking, his lips distended like a camel's.

Maybe my love was not a red, red rose, but a red, red maple instead. I was in it for the long haul, but may not have seemed to anyone the right guy over the short haul. Maybe that's what Alice Harron missed when she sensed that I was not grinding myself into the mud with real conviction. It is true I could have shouted a bit louder at the passing locomotives, drawn up the shout from the bottom of my belly somewhere like Mario Lanza, but that's all hindsight.

What was I to offer Bunny in her young age? Was I to sit with her on a couch, the lights way down low, and give her an insightful reading of *Hamlet* or *Going after Cacciato*? Would she flip happily with me through the sad pages of a Diane Arbus photo collection? Could I ask her to park her little aerodynamic pick-me-up job of a car alongside my clunky Oldsmobile? What did I have to give her? The quick and easy recipe for gaspacho, clipped from the evening paper? A stroll down the sunny streets of suburban Toronto? A theory about the decline of the dollar against the mark and yen? Decaffeinated Earl Grey tea? A brand new 50 to 120 millimeter Minolta lens bought at a 15% employee discount? A rubdown with aromatic oil after a long night at the lounge? Yogurt-covered raisins? And would there be a sombrero for her, too, at the airport when we greeted my parents, and silver-plated candlesticks at our shower, and discount coupons pinned to our clipboard for an oil change at Mr. Lube? Would our subversive activities draw us into the dark world of radar busters below our dashboard and cable splitters for our TVs and a bill for an extra drink at the lounge tossed in among our tax receipts? A salute to war veterans at the Veterans' Parade? Sparklers on our birthday cake? Hurrahs during the Stanley Cup playoffs? A quick bout of love after a rushed reading of *Sticky Days in Tahiti*? A clean night under the stars at Algonquin Park? The do-wa-diddy sounds of the golden oldies? The solitary call of the loon? The last scraps of day-old crullers for the departing geese?

A rustling of leaves behind me startled me. It was nothing but a sparrow, as it turned out, but it drove me out from behind the bush. I marched like Patton across the lawn and up the three steps to the Lopez door.

There, I could hear the plaintive, small voice of a woman. "Why don't you just forget about her? You *know* that she is not here. I don't hear from her like before."

I peeked inside to see a woman, even smaller than her voice, with her arm around a teenage girl. They were standing in the living room with Almond! There were teacups behind them on a wooden table with an embroidered tablecloth.

"You must know where she went," he said. "How far could she have gotten to?"

"Michael, I've told you everything I know. She said she was leaving for a while, and she would be in touch." I stepped in as quietly as I could.

"Did she leave with someone? You *have* to tell me." Almond was standing even closer to the Lopezes now. She pulled her daughter more tightly to her.

"She left with someone. The last time I saw her she was with a man with a big, red car. He had black hair and a nice jacket."

"Goddamn it," Almond said, running his hand back through his own black hair.

"Don't curse in my house, please, Michael."

Then the young girl piped up, "Yeah, why don't you just get lost! Can't you even take a hint of something?"

Almond stepped closer to the pair. "You are just like your sister, do you know that, Maria?" He had his hand on her shoulder.

I had ready my Peter Lorre gangster voice, but it broke into a squeak half way through. "Is that a good thing or a bad thing, Almon*etti*?" I peeped.

Almond turned to look at me. The lumps on our heads were aimed directly at each other like chrome bumpers. "Oh, here he is again," Almond said with fury in his eyes. "Bunny's little guardian angel."

He lunged at me, then all at once his head bucked, and he fell unconscious against my chest before sliding to the floor. Maria stood behind him, holding a large, green crystal bowl with gaudy wings sticking out of it. She put her hand up to her mouth and smiled as if she'd burped. "Excuse us," I said, and dragged Almond out the door and down the little steps. Maria and her mother followed me to the door. Maria smiled; then her mother pulled her into the house, closing the door tight and locking it behind them.

The cab driver didn't flinch as I struggled to pull Almond across the lawn to the car. "Can we throw him in the back?" I asked, panting.

He looked at me with tired eyes. "I'll have to charge you for a piece of luggage," he said.

"It's a deal," I said. The driver opened the trunk of the cab, but I had meant the back seat, so he helped me wedge him into it.

Chapter Eighteen

By the time we dropped Almond off at The Way of
Life Assembly of God Church and sped along toward the
hotels, I'd almost forgotten about him. All I could think
of was the red car that had picked up Bunny.

There was no one in the hotel room — what else was
new? — but Clyde's suitcase was packed and it stood by
the door. Now, I have had low points in my life, but this
one sank me to the bottom of the ocean with an anvil
chained to my ankle. I was hot with rage and at the same
time felt weak as a noodle. I trudged around aimlessly,
pausing now and then to look at the silent TV cabinet with
"all the entertainment in the world" bursting to get out. I
took my sweet time swinging into action. I took a long,
slow shower, and meticulously packed my things. I went
down, swung around the corner to look from a distance
for the happy doorman at the Taj Mahal, waved excitedly
as he saluted, and sat one last time on a dark bench on the
Boardwalk directly across from Irene's, "Atlantic City's
Oldest Boardwalk Gift Shop."

Good old Irene — standing stalwart through thick and
thin with her day-glo T-shirts and proud little plastic
bubbles of the City under water but with flecks of snow
flying around in them. I wondered if Irene had been

around back when good old Charlie had had his engagement ring flung in his face down on Chicken Bone Beach.

Then I made my move. It took me no time to find the Blackjack Warrior in the casino, saying, "Hit me," but half-asleep, barely noticing what cards were hitting him.

"Doing well, Clyde?" Rage warbled in my throat.

"Oh, hi," he said, smiling up at me groggily. "I just thought I'd get in a few more hands before we took off out of here."

"Are we driving into the night?" I asked.

"Why not?" he said. "The old warrior's had his fill of pillage and plunder on this little voyage. I'm pretty much ready to blow this popsicle stand. I would have left this morning, so I came to get you at the hospital, but you'd taken off." Clyde turned his cards over and tossed them forward. There was a woman, sitting three seats over, wearing a feather in her diamond hair band and a glittering diamond necklace.

"Well, I hope I didn't worry your pretty little head," I said.

"Not at all," he said.

"I'd like to have a word with you, Bob, if I may."

Clyde narrowed his eyes as he looked up at me. "OK, in a minute," he said.

"*Now.*"

The glittering woman looked over at us. The dealer didn't flinch. This was a city of non-flinchers, if I'd ever seen one. I put a hand on Clyde's shoulder and squeezed hard.

"What the hell's the matter with you?" Clyde said, swatting my hand away. I glared back at him. "Hold my place here for a minute," he said to the dealer. "I'll be right back."

Clyde followed me up to a pillar by the entrance, and then I turned on him. "Where's Bunny?"

"How in the hell should I know?"

I closed in on him. "What'd you do with her?"

"What?" he said, glancing at the bump on my head. I grabbed his shoulders and pinned him up against the pillar.

"In your goddamn red car! When you picked her up at her mother's place!"

"That was *days* ago!" he said, still in my grip. "That was the night you met her!" There was fear in his face. I could read it like a billboard. I had never before seen fear in Clyde's face.

"What kind of a snake are you?" I still gripped his shoulders and was poised to raise my knee into his crotch. "Tell me some more about Alice Harron." I pushed him against the pillar. "Tell me about Jane and Jeffy! Tell me about Pretti, with an '*i*'! Tell me some of your lies, Clyde! Tell me about *sleeping with Bunny*."

"Yes, I *slept* with her," he said. I shot my fist dead toward his nose, but Clyde caught it in mid-air and twisted it until I was down on one knee. "The night you met her, I *slept* with her," he said, gazing down at me. "The next night she was in that weird trance, and I *slept* again *beside* her, just as soon as I got through sleeping *biblically* with the lovely Pretti with an '*i*', and I might add she makes a terrific *sleeping* mate, that Pretti with an '*i*.'" He hoisted me to my feet with surprising strength and dusted off the jacket of his that I was wearing. I was ready to pound him, but this time he caught both my fists and held them.

"What the hell is your problem anyway, Eddie?"

"Don't you get it?" I said. "I'm the one who's always there for everyone. I'm always the one at the airport to pick up people and the one at the club to rescue hypnotized people and the one who's there building the snowman with Jeffy, and you're always the one who picks up the spoils."

"If you don't want to do those things," he said, "you shouldn't. No one's making you. But don't *do* them and then go around saying 'woe is me' the rest of your life."

I burst into tears. Clyde stood and watched me for a while and then he said, "I'm sorry, little guy," and hugged me. "I'm sorry things didn't work out for you here."

We stayed that way for a moment until Clyde realized what he was doing, his eyes suddenly darting all around as he let go of me. "Why don't we check out?" he said. "You go get our bags, and I'll take care of the bill."

As I walked out the door — the wrong door, the back one, leading again to the Boardwalk — I was drained and quivering like a baby. I pulled myself together as well as I could when it occurred to me that I hadn't gotten Jeffy anything, so I staggered over to Irene's. I pulled out Junior Monopoly for him from among some dusty boxes of Parcheesi and magnetic Travel Checkers and wandered back, passing right by smiling Merv, until a miracle occurred before my eyes: Desmond Pencil stood in the lobby, counting some change in his hand.

"Desmond!" I called out to him. "Can it be you?"

Pencil didn't smile at me. Charm was never his long suit.

"Eddie?" he said. "Markson?"

"Yes, *Eddie*. What are you *doing* here, for heaven's sake?"

"Why, I have as much right to be here as anyone."

"Of course you do," I said. "But I've been thinking about you constantly. I've been worrying about you — *dreaming* about you even, for cripe's sake."

"Eddie, I never knew," he said, "that you were . . . you know, that way."

"I'm not that way — no — it's not that. Listen," I said as I dropped my bag and gripped his shoulders. He winced and stepped back, so I stepped forward. "Listen, call me sometime, Des," I told him. "Walk by my place — I mean, *come* by."

"OK, Eddie, I will." He was studying the bump on my head. In fact, he was talking directly to it. "I will, I promise."

I was grinning broadly, but Desmond seemed not to know that was his cue to smile back. I loosened my grip, retrieved my bag and galloped to the elevator. As I stepped on, I wondered if I should go down to the casino to toss some dice but thought, no, there be something better for me upstairs — I have had an authentic sighting of Desmond Pencil!

When I found nothing in our room, my spirits drooped until I turned again to close the door and spotted an envelope that had been slipped under it. It was marked, "EDDIE — PRIVATE." I sat on Clyde's bed and tore it open.

Dearest Eddie,

I couldn't find you guys and didn't want to run out on you so I decided to write you this note. I'll try to watch my english here too a little because I know your a serious student of those things Eddie. I'm leaving here for a while. I'll take my show on the road I guess see what jobs I can land. Maybe I'll even end up back in Canada sometime. Life has been kind of complicated lately as maybe you can tell. I know that it sounds like running away but I think sometimes that its the only real way back when you run for a while and understand what you've left behind. Including you now, it looks like. You and your older brother are really very sweet in your own ways and I have a feeling I'll miss you alot but maybe it won't be for that long at all and things will sort themselves out I'm sure. I'll miss you both. Thanks for everything you did for me Eddie and don't be two hard on Clyde, he does his best in his own way and has his heart in the right place. Tell him good bye. I'll read the badge of courage I promise. I like you so much.

xo
Bunny

Chapter Nineteen

Clyde asked me to drive. He took a camel look at his *My Fair Lady* tape, then glanced around the dashboard and felt under his seat for a moment in search of his other tapes before sitting back. He looked over at me. "Hey, are you wearing Brut or Musk or some damn thing?"

"Nope."

A minute later he was asleep. He slept even through the first fill-up, and I found myself happy not to have to talk to anyone, except for one stretch of road just outside Philadelphia when I nearly ran off the road because I realized I'd forgotten *Sticky Days in Tahiti* in the Gideon Bible drawer! Even worse, I still hadn't found out what happened to poor, old Henry Fleming, my Civil War pal.

I found some staticky opera on the radio — Rossini, I think it was — and settled back happily in the luxurious seat of the Allanté. It was not until we drove past Allentown, Pennsylvania, that I began worrying that we might have been heading the wrong way and would have to settle down among the Amish. I woke Clyde an hour later and suggested we stop for some coffee and a doughnut. As I held the door for him, Clyde wiped his groggy face.

We ordered and, at the cash, when I was pinching out

napkins from the dispenser, Clyde said, "Can you spot me a couple of bucks?"

"Sure," I said and fished out a hundred.

We found ourselves a corner table and sat in the swiveling chairs. "I forgot to tell you," he said, reaching into his pocket, "there was a note for you at the desk when I checked out."

He handed me the small, sealed envelope. It had the address and number of the Taj Mahal printed on it, and the familiar upside-down minaret as its back flap.

Clyde sipped noisily from his hot coffee. "It's OK," he said, "I don't mind. Open it."

"Did Bunny leave you a note, too?"

"No, she didn't. And her name's not Bunny," he said. "It's Penny Lopez. Did you know that?"

"It *is*?" I took a sharply pointed, whistling slurp from my own coffee and wondered when she had told him that and whether he'd asked her or she'd simply volunteered the information. But one thing was certain: just when you think you know someone best, he fires out a volley which can knock you straight out of your newly darned socks.

Clyde lost interest in the note — or maybe he was just giving me a break — and trudged off to the bathroom. The note was supposed to be from Bunny, but Clyde's familiar, cardiogram handwriting was unmistakable:

Dear Eddie,

Sorry I had to run out on you at the hospital, but things got a bit too heated between you and Clyde who is, after all, not such a bad guy — don't be too hard on him.

Come back to Atlantic City sometime and maybe we can get it on. Bring Clyde and I'll bring Pretti. Drive safely.
Love ya,
Bunny

Clyde came out of the bathroom and said, "Let's go," without looking at me. He also forgot to ask what was in the note. We made our way out to the car, he unlocked all the doors with a flick of the key, tossed me the keys and got in on the passenger side. I saw a look on his face at the beginning of a grin, but he turned away before going into one.

Just before we pulled out of the service station, I had a good, long look at the map and felt I could pretty well navigate the rest of the way home. Clyde fell asleep again almost immediately. With his back to me, he looked small in the fading light, and crumpled like a bug. After a few minutes, I thought I saw him shiver, though it could well have been the shaking of the car. Just in case, I reached over into the back, got hold of his jacket by the sleeve and pulled it up front over his shoulder. I considered for a moment how it was the peacock bore its young. I wondered if there was some other way besides laying eggs or having them live. Maybe little peacocks sprang from their mother's head, bursting with feathers, the way Athena sprang from her father's. I decided it was something I never wanted to look up.

Then I felt I was having one of those out-of-body experiences, like a big wide-angle shot from the air, capturing two dark specks in a red car, set against the light of the harvest moon.